The Vine Keeper

MESSAGES
IN POETRY & PROSE

William S. Peters, Sr.

Credits

Author
William S. Peters, Sr.

Edited by
Alan W. Jankowski

Foreword by
Dr. Peter C. Rogers, D.D., Ph.D.

Compiled by
Janet P. Caldwell

Cover Design
Chyna Blue
Edyfyin' Grapix
&
William S. Peters, Sr.

General Information

The Vine Keeper
Messages in Poetry & Prose

William S. Peters, Sr.
1st Edition : 2012

This Publishing is protected under Copyright Law as a "Collection". All rights for all submissions are retained by the Individual Author and or Artist. No part of this Publishing may be Reproduced, Transferred in any manner without the prior **WRITTEN CONSENT** of the "Material Owner" or it's Representative Inner Child Press. Any such violation infringes upon the Creative and Intellectual Property of the Owner pursuant to International and Federal Copyright Law. Any queries pertaining to this "Collection" should be addressed to Publisher of Record.

Publisher Information

1st Edition : Inner Child Press
innerchildpress@gmail.com
www.innerchildpress.com

This Collection is protected under U.S. and International Copyright Laws

Copyright © 2012 : 1-827276301

ISBN-13 : 978-0615700649
ISBN-10 : 0615700640

$ 29.95

Cover Design :   Chyna Blue of Edyfyin' Graphix & William S. Peters, Sr.

*Nightmares and Dreams are both Card Carrying,
Dues Paying Members of the same Laborer's Union . . .
"ME"*

william s. peters, sr.

Dedication

i dedicate this collection of my expressions to

all the beautiful souls like you . . .

The Community of Humanity . . .

~ familia mea ~

~

cogito ergo sum

Je pense donc je suis

René Descartes

31 March 1596 ~ 11 February 1659

Reconciliation has a price that most are not willing to pay . . . one must be willing to look at their Past, and give all or their Drama, Fear, Doubts and Judgment away . . . yes we must empty the purse of Self and experience what it is to be poor of our Character of yesterday that we may build new Houses on the strong unwavering Foundations of Virtue.

william s. peters, sr.

Preface

On the pages to come, awaits a journey as expressed through my verse. The words reflect an experiential-ness of my own and one that many of us at some level have had.

The Vine Keeper is perhaps somewhat an "Egoic" examination of my inner self, my "Inner Child" and addresses many of the recurring questions and perhaps insights i may have had, or at least i thought i have had in my 'Life Path'. Poetry for me as well as many others who i commune with tends to be the foundation of our Soul-felt reflections, our Emotions and the things we Think.

One of my cherished quotes comes from the French Philosopher Descartes' who coined the phrase 'cogito ergo sum' (i think therefore i am). Though many who read my work may defer in part or in its entirety from my perspectives, but what i must say is this . . . they are honest and therefore "Authentic" considerations of Creation, Life from most times a subjective point of view, and sometimes on rare occasions i touch on some things that may appear to be detached or quasi-objective.

Throughout my life of wonder and discovery, my chief gripe perhaps would have been this. we are not taught to think creatively or independently of the machine. In The Vine Keeper i try. I hope, that this offering does justice to that dynamic which spawns you, the reader to look beyond the containment and remove the surreal lines in the Sand we think corral us.

Blessed Be

Bill
inner child

*the more i move "me" out of the equation,
the more i discover myself . . .*

william s. peters, sr.

Foreword

If you know anything about wine, you know that the quality of grapes determine the superiority of the wine more so than any other factor. And while there are many contributing influences to the grape's quality such as; weather conditions, soil, minerals, acidity, time of harvest and pruning methods, none are more important than that of "The Vine Keeper's" keen sense of knowledge and understanding of what makes for the perfect grape.

Depending on which source you use, there is roughly anywhere from 600,000 to 900,000 words in the English language with each word containing its own vibration and feeling tone. As a writer, I understand the importance of choosing the precise word at the precise time in order to convey the right tone or essence. As a Wordsmith, it is very important to know and recognize how choosing the right concoction of words, similar to that of the Vine Keeper choosing just the right grapes, is crucial to effectively convey ideas from one mind to the next. And as a poet, this selective process of pruning, cutting and clipping words from the abundant reservoir of 600,000 to 900,000 possible choices is even more critical. Speaking to this; I can recall meeting with William Peters Sr., affectionately known as "Just Bill" to me in May of 2012 and having this very conversation. He a poet, among many other things, and I a writer, discovered that we each share a fondness for word use and its significance for communication. As we walked down the bustling Hollywood strip in Los Angeles California with the Sun to our backs and dusk on the horizon, nothing else existed other than the bond we shared through our deep, heartfelt conversation and musings over how important choosing the right word can be.

In this wonderful, masterful anthology of deep introspections of poetry and prose, Bill serves as the true Keeper of the Vine with his meticulous choice of only the finest grapes of savory meaning and stirring inspiration. His words being the fruits of his mental labor and his soul's yearnings, prompts us each to ponder the unfathomable aspects of being while imbibing his intoxicating literary prose which literary oozes from your lips as you read it.

One cannot merely read these words; you have to drink them in. And you cannot take too much in too quickly, for you must stop to savor the sweet, melodic flavor of each hand-picked word. If you've ever read the work of 13th Century poet Rumi or the Italian poet Dante of the Middle Ages or The Song of Solomon or the ancient Indian Vedas, or any other divinely inspired text, one cannot help but to place Bill among the echelon of these fine literary giants. Just reading his words invokes deep contemplation and an inner sense of profound introspection and retrospection simultaneously. Prepare your mind and palate to receive a delectable, mouthwatering, savory, moving, stirring, stimulating and thought provoking jolt of the perfect blend of just the right words meticulously placed in just the right places.

Namaste,

Dr. Peter C. Rogers, D.D., Ph.D.

Dr. Peter C. Rogers, D.D., Ph.D., is a Light-Worker, a Life Coach, Motivational Speaker, Minister of Metaphysics and Spiritual Counselor. He is the author of *Ultimate Truth: Book I*, *Universal Truth: Thinking Outside the Box: Book II* and the up and coming *One Hundred Disciplines to Higher Consciousness: A Conclusive Synopsis on Spiritual Principles*.

Dr. Rogers is a skilled lecturer and teacher of the Master Key System. He teaches an extensive class and has appeared on several shows to present this ancient system of manifestation formulated by Charles F. Haanel over 100 years ago. In 2010, Dr. Rogers founded a spiritual counseling practice called **TRUTH Dynamics** to help assist people in their quest for self realization. Currently, he serves as the president of a Non-Profit organization called P.E.L.S.A which he and his wife formed in 2006 to assist people in overcoming addiction. Dr. Rogers has been a student of Spirituality and Metaphysics for the past 20 years and in 2009, he received a Doctorate of Divinity in Spiritual Counseling as well as a Doctorate of Philosophy in Metaphysics from The University of Metaphysical Sciences. He currently resides in Long Beach, California where he continues to devote his time and energy writing, lecturing and mentoring others on their spiritual journey towards higher consciousness.

Contact Information

Telephone : 323.270.7737

Web Site : http://ultimatetruthbooks.com/

Standing in the wilderness shouting

I am here, arms wide open
Waiting on my creator to
Speak
Talk
Move
Give
Me something for you
So that I can be obedient
To fall on my knees in fasting
Eating only the words of
Life
Death
Birth
Stillness
With all the power of first
And all the waiting of last
Beginning and end
The words of the crafter
Poet
Writer
Lyricist
Deliverer
And I will ink it quick
Placing it everywhere you are
So that you can see and hear
What is in store for you
Me
They
Us
All
There is never a time
When the word was not offered
Only when it was not received
And not called forth to teach
Truth
Wisdom
Correction
Love
For that is our purpose
And why were made
And what we have been
Ordered to spread among
Ghettos
Cities
Fields
Hearts
Til all has been healed I remain
Jusbill in the Wilderness

by Gail Shaz

sometimes life is like a Blind Man trying to teach a Dog how to read Chinese . . . some days are like that aren't they ? . . . no one gets it . . . not even the proposed Teacher . . . so me, i just STOP, Reflect and have me a Smile and a Chuckle . . . that always makes it better and transmutes the occasion into a worthy experience.

william s. peters, sr.

Table of Contents

The Vine Keeper	1
poetry is my prayer	7
a letter to the Universe . . . i apologize	11
blinded by the light	16
a Father's Prayer to Father	18
and i pray	21
beyond	23
a certain destruction to come	24
a Solemn Morning Chill	28
i am . . . absolved	29
Aquarius	33
but a breath away	35
and the parade begins	40
as i am alone	44
Compellation and Tryst	46
can you hear that call ?	50
at the cross	52
close our eyes	57
can you do that for me . . . it only cost a dollar down the street	62
all is one big Ocean	65
created in the image . . . so act like one	68
but a test you say	72
chasing	75
but I'm not sure it's poetic	80
Cogito Ergo Sum	81

Table of Contents... continued

Chaos	84
again . . . i've been here before	89
a parent's tears . . . a parent's fears	92
born on the Fourth of July	96
again today	98
but the letting go	99
and i ask	104
and that i am	107
this is why I sleep . . .	109
Vision Quest	110
We speak beautiful things	111
us for breakfast	112
who am i	117
Today i lost my faith	120
we believed	126
the Perfect People Poem	134
won't you climb with me	135
they are people . . . too	137
the World that is becoming Real	140
you are 2 dammmmed	142
Tomorrow Perhaps	143
well . . .	148
yet we shine	151
They would have a King	153
Ultimately	158
The visions of a fool	162

Table of Contents... continued

the universe replete, thus i speak	164
the words	170
the Saints Walk By	171
Utopic Dreams ~ a Memorial Day Salute	173
there are small slivers of light	179
what we are becoming	183
what is this soft voice i hear	186
to be who i am	187
without tears	189
who really understands ?	192
Today i Teach	195
the road	196
would we do it ?	197
they were right	200
will that do for you ?	204
what i am	211
this is a dumb ass poem for dumb ass people	217
this crushed heart	218
the widow	221
the storm is coming	223
what it is	226
i stand not alone	229
last night i sat and i asked myself	230
metaphorically speaking	233
let us party	239
my love for you	241

Table of Contents... continued

i want my poetry to . . .	242
love did me in again	246
i am listening	248
is it lunch time yet	250
i hear you	251
Metaphoric dreams	253
of course i said it	256
just a write, a right	261
Mount Kyllini	264
i still see demons	266
again	269
my brother I come to you	270
Monsters in my closet	271
i serve the silence	274
I am listening to 'now'	277
losing the battle . . .	281
not any more	284
if i held your truth . . . my resolution	288
i am he	290
measuring things	297
of life	298
"I am thankful"	300
I remember in the beginning	303
it's all possible . . . isn't it	304
i don't want to dance no more	307

Table of Contents... continued

do you know the way to wonderland ?	309
fly anyway, it's a good death . . .	311
his expectations were dying	313
Happy New Year	316
Glass Houses	318
Home . . . come	319
eat one	324
grey days	326
every day	328
disturbing my conversation with my muse ?	331
did you take the Red Pill or the Blue one ?	334
happily here after	339
Daydreaming again	341
Flowers in the Wind	344
here on the ground	345
Don't you ?	347
fractured disconnectedness . . .	349
Heaven again	352
do we understand	353
Damn Muses . . . gotta love them	356
Grandma says	358
est tempus	360
damaged goods	363
Half Moon Light, Half Moon Dark	369

Table of Contents... continued

i am a Souldier	372
dancing with delusional libidos	373
divine expression	376
Faith	380
of things in a frame	384
in flight . . . and the music played	387
so they say	390
~ * ~ the Jester ~ * ~	394

Epilogue

a few words from Bill	399
a few words from Janet	401
a few words from Shareef Abdur-Rasheed	403
a few words from Regina Ann	405
a few words from Martina Reisz Newberry	407
a few words from Bill Douglas	409
a few words from Teresa E. Gallion	411

The Vine Keeper

MESSAGES
IN POETRY & PROSE

William S. Peters, Sr.

*i have always said. . .
a good poem is one that corrals the mind of the reader
and leaves the gate open.*

william s. peters, sr.

the Vine Keeper

here sit i
in the Holiest of Holies
the Vine-keeper
embracing the passage of time
as she marches forth to harvest

i have nurtured the soils
of this garden
with a labor of love
and quiet expectation

my hands which knead forth promise
are covered with the fragrance of the earth
whose thirst is filled
by the sweat of my brow

i have exacted my duty
and continue so
through
that of the morrow
with an unrivaled love
that i may press the fruits
of my labor
to make a new wine
worthy of anointing
the lips of my Lorde,
for i am the Vine-keeper
and this is my charge

There is the sound of footprints
gracefully dancing upon my ear
"who goes there" i cry
and a voice volumous
and splendorous replies
"it is i, thy servant"

i understood not this speaking
for it was the voice of my Lorde
and i fall upon the ground
my face turned to the earth
as a reverent-type fear
comes upon my entire essence
and consumes me
like a ravenous plague of plenty
for the Source of my being
my Progenitor Father
approaches

He bids me to rise
but i can not
of my own accord
nor may i look upon His presence
so i avert my eyes
as i realize
that i have been summoned
and sanctified
and all about me
i defied
for it, the world
has lost all import

i ask
Father, what would you have me do
how may i serve thee
name the task
for i am yours to command
please demand of me
that i may see
thy will

i pray i understand

and He spake unto me
with a certain sanctity of enmity
that stills the rush of life
all about me
and within me

He said to me
"Servant"
i have come
to eat of the labor
of thy love for me
give of me thine heart
which is mine
oh Vine Keeper

i humbled myself
for the flatterous embrace
of his words
ushered forth a pride
that i could not hide

i beamed brightly
for the light of his
which resides inside me
in my spirit
cause my heart to beat
with a fervor
and He and i
could hear it

i could feel an anticipatory longing
that manifested to my consciousness
as a holy song
as played from the strings of
a Holy Harp
like that of the Angels
who gather round the Throne
playing a music the day long
and the voice of my Lorde spoke
and said unto me
"I have come to eat of the labor of thy love for me"
"I have come for your fruit"
Feed me thy best
but know ye this . . .

Plumbs i have had
Pomegranates too
Apples have i had
but now i come to you
to satisfy the sum
of my longings

i come hither
to not taste of the bitter
but that of my wantings
and whimsical hauntings
to be filled
as i taste of the fruit
of thy tilled and nurtured garden

the spoils of thy soils,
i have come for the fruit
of thy Vine
that sweetest of grape
that has ravaged and raped
my senses
with a promise elated
yet not sated
won't you feed me,
feed your Lorde
thy faithful servant

Upon his request
i found myself speechless
and speak . . . i could not

i could not mutter
nor utter
a word to be heard

all of me
was twisted
caught in this cataclysmic
state of orgasmic ecstasy
for the best of me
had just been revealed unto me

i was seeing
feeling
the death of me
the old me
as a verity of my life
came unto me
and graced me
with a surety
unrivaled by any means

this is what i had always
vied for
cried for
and this day
i shall die for
and i deny it no more
for
i am but a servant
in the vineyard
a Vine Keeper
in the Garden of my Lorde

poetry is my prayer

my poetry is my prayer
for understanding
that i may comprehend
the beauty and the pain
the crazy and the sane

i write for clarity
to end my disparity
with my world about me
and about you too

i write to examine
that which troubles me
or to share my joys

there are sometimes insights
and lights to brighten our nights
and some times there are stars
revealing life scars
that assists me
in seeing far
down my road
and that which i left behind

poetry helps me clear my mind
my spirit
my emotions
there are songs playing
can you hear it

can you feel the motion
of love as she beckons you
beckons me
to reconcile
our differences

poetry,
you have to love her
she teaches
she preaches
she breeches topics
we would rather not indulge in
and some we are all too eager
to divulge in
she beseeches us
to look closely
at our Sins and our Blessings

through poetry our souls get to confessing
that which was once a burden
that then becomes
our wing fitted verse

we disperse our essence
like presents
in syllables and words
to be read
to be heard

they are laced with
adverbs and adjectives
nouns, verbs and prepositions
and such

some times enough
some times too much

we give to you our Soul's expletives
and thoughts we have deleted
if you can read between the lines
and find our deeper meanings

some of our stanzas are lyrical
some rhyme
in some sort of way
whether obvious
or ambiguous
there is a greater gift
to be held
by he who has an ear
or an eye

sometimes poetry calls for us
to shed a tear
cry
face our fears
die
put on our armor
vie
see our self
deny
be courageous
try

but never should we lie
especially to our own soul
for it will not hold
up

we need to
send those poetic expressions up
my friend
just like you do your prayers
for that is what poetry is
another prayer
request
bequest
conquest
to the universe
as we divest ourselves
of that which troubles our waters
to exact a certain beauty
only found in the duty
written
sketched
drawn quarters
of what poetry
can do

poetry is my prayer

a letter to the Universe . . . i apologize

i apologize for being less than what i am
for the lies i told myself
for trying to be someone else

i apologize for all the wasted prayers
the begging for the things
that would mask my fears
in forgetfulness
and i apologize for my doubts
about the power that resides
inside me

i apologize for the blaming of circumstances
those i claimed were beyond my control
for in truth i knew deep in my soul
that i was the creator of these things
yet i acted from a point of powerlessness
i apologize

i apologize for keeping my eyes shut
closed to my realities
of my abilities to overcome
instead i decided
to piss and moan
and i chided you, Universe
asking you to override
the decisions i made
to hide
i apologize

i apologize for not speaking out
when i was confronted
many times
i spoke not
and i did flee to this paper and pen
to exact rhymes
about my life's angst
and the things
i felt stood against
my integrity
i apologize

i apologize
for my lack of faith in the unseen
i apologize for all the times i was mean
to others
to you
to my own being
i apologize

i apologize for the karma i needlessly collected
yes i was the proverbial garbage man
of the universe
the Fred Sanford of Soul
doing not the things you told me
and you tolerated me
held me still
and scolded me not
yes
i apologize

*i apologize
for all those tears
those tears i shed for you
those tears i shed for me
those tears that flooded
the treasure chambers of my dreams
with non-belief
and frustrations
and disdain
and indifference
i apologize
i apologize for all the children
all the children's innocent desires for joy
the ones ignored
starting with that of my own
and i have always known
that the seeds sown
yielded the fruit we had to eat
yet i planted the seeds of malcontent
in your Universal and Cosmic Mind
just the same
in the name of me
in the name of you
in the name of some God i never knew
i apologize*

*i apologize for not paying attention
i apologize for pouting and my dissension
my dissension from the way
of the days past
those to come
and my now
and somehow though
i know you understand and are forgiving*

i apologize for not being able to do so
yes i apologize for my frailties
for i was not created in such a manner
i apologize

i apologize for usurping your plans for me
many times it was my selfishness
but certainly
it was me
who chose not to see
things your way
and that sanity
that sanctity
i sought
could not be bought
and i apologize for trying to do so
anyway
i apologize

and finally

i apologize for this note to you
for in my clueless meandering
this is my attempt to reconcile
all the denials
through all my trials
and tribulations
that you were my answer
that part of you that makes me a dancer
of the sheer joys to be here
and for holding to fear
instead of my light
and though this may be the beginning
of the end of my night

know that
i will not apologize no more
for sure
for right now i am walking through that door
that tells me that "i am" that "I AM"
and like you Father Source
of course
i have the power to "Be"
what ever i wish to "BE"
and i shall do my thing
for the Universe in me.

and that's my letter to you
Universe . . . i love you
as you love me
i apologize

blinded by the light

being blinded by Doctrine

poisoned by rote

he depended on the

"how you feel" syndrome

the veil starting losing its substance

many years ago

the visual soul connections

existed not for him

circumspection

nor reflection

served a meaningful purpose

to support the hierarchy of man

for the fabric of belief

just would not bond

to that plane

of indifferent acquiescence

of the people

lessons were plentiful

for those who would look

but most would not

they were too disturbing

and required commitment

to the shit meant

to empower us

to get up off our ass for change

we would rather rearrange our inconvenient virtues

our values

those which tend to annoy us to a point

to where we feel guilty

stealing our power divine

a Father's Prayer to Father

Father,
i am tired
i am weary
and through my tear-laden eyes
i cry to you

had there been no You
there would be no me

this road of Trials and Tribulations
is daunting
and still yet
my past is haunting me
begging for reconciliation
back to you
and i know You knew
i would come to this

but another kiss
is all i desire

to feel Thy lips upon my own
affirming that some
of my sown Seed
will produce a sweet fruit

in my many times of desolation
you have pulled me through
with naught but your Silence
and hence i now affirm it all

those prayers have been answered
for here i am
with another day
to make a way
like David
my brother
to your heart
only to find out
i have never left

yet my quest
to navigate
through my own delusions
continue

the Wilderness has been good to me
for i did find …
most of me
and all of You
for as the Son spoke
the yoke is not easy,
but if you need me
"There I AM"

Cleave a wood …
turn over a rock
through all without
all within
call me
for i am thy friend
as i said
"There I Am"

e'en before Abraham

damn . . .
why did it take so long
for me to remember this song ?

a God-less life
is no life at all
it is but death eternal
a never ending
self induced purgatory

so i as a Father Pray
this Prayer to my Father

and i pray

a brisk breeze comes
a cold front embraces life
accompanied by an unusual rain

the sky is half clear
and the other half
seriously overcast
even nature appears
to be confused

is this a sign
of a coming
age
where ice may recapture
the balance of mother

what are we to do ?
gather matches
and pray
that a wind not come
and extinguish our flame
the one we have left
unattended

yesterday
was balmy
i conjured visions
of sandy beaches
and pleasant escapes
from a looming reality
i smiled profusely
within that room
filled with funny shaped
and curved mirrors
serving my reflective delusions

i am now haunted
within a consciousness
that i would rather put aside
hide from
and to sum it all up
i write an open ended poem
and i pray

beyond

i pay homage

for the journey of man

my hopes are pinned

to his return

home

for in his arms

he carries bounty

in his mind

he carries memories

in his heart

he carries wisdom

in his spirit

there is wonder

and we all will share

simply

because he journeyed

beyond

a certain destruction to come

i have thrown my hands in the air a million times
expressing my frustration
pertaining the destructive propensities
of man

the war wages on

the once felt pains
the anguish i once bore
is not a numbed experience
i live just to feel
that occasional tingle
evidencing hope

i know, the logic is twisted

long lost brothers
whose Fathers were brothers as well
vying for their blood
to be spilled
that they may mix and dance
in the soils of anguish
of all the Mother's tears
leaving a legacy
a lore
that the Children to come
yearn to exceed
more death
more destruction

i never did understand war
hate
bias
nor indifference
but through the years
i have used them as tools as well
i could blame it on
the conditioning
and my non-seditious embrace of it
though i never quite acquiesced
the taste of it

there are countless Holocausts
and countless 911's
that man has endured throughout the ages
that snuck in and out of the pages of history
with alias' and pseudonyms

mindless megalomaniacal murderers
we call "Heads of State"
and other such lofty titles
think nothing of the common people
their homes
their families
their culture
their villages
nor their souls
maybe Clinton had the right idea . . .

i walk down the pathway of crumbled bricks
which used to be the street where i lived
where children once played
laughing and smiling
and offering to the universe

their glee

those precious moments
still live in me
for i was one of them

perhaps it is all in the growing up
it does come too fast
and then we are dead
just when we think we have a hold on it
life

i somehow sense there is a greater time to come
when we actually will
as an insensitive humanity
succeed
in our destructive proclivity

for our civility
is now held at ransom
by an economy and laws
that support our ultimate demise

don't be surprised
for when it was time for us to vote
we were either sleeping
or inebriated by our desires
for keeping up
with some proverbial Jones Family
and now, even the Jones are out on the street
begging for understanding
solace and peace
a job and a bite to eat
even a Happy Meal will do

but even Ronald has been pimped out
turned out
just like us

funny the illness we have allowed
promulgated
to feed our children
is so mildly accepted
and we smile
deceptively
in the face of the looming death
that encircles the globe
and our hearts
choking our hopes

in truth i think that we do know
that death is a necessary journey
we must take
before resurrection

and in our own way
we welcome . . .

a certain destruction to come

a Solemn Morning Chill

it was a Solemn June Morning

disguising itself as late Autumn

seeking not to reveal its fair countenance

that a Summer day often gives to the world

i abandoned the shorts i donned

for a pair of Jeans

and a long sleeve shirt

no questions

just a chill

that needed to be addressed

arrested

without contest

i am … absolved

the Demons of Darkness
are dancing with glee
for the Children
have not yet fully awakened

the bells on the Steeple
are still ringing
calling home all who have forsaken
their Cosmic Birthright
in the midst of this night
adorned with things
which ushers forth the grande delusion

and the collusion betwixt the fallen
the conspiracy
found within their heresy
has stifled the sound
the sound of the calling
which we have been waiting for
for so many eons

my soul is screaming
let us arise
let us get up
let us dance in the night
let us dance in the light
of the distant memories
and the faintly twinkling Stars
and the liquid luminescence of the Moon
let us dance the dance
of a truth

that is not moved
and is not soothed
by the smooth tongues of deceit

let us speak that word
known only to the Great Soul
that which resides within me
that word
that has not been heard
since "Life's Tree"
has been planted in the Garden

and
by the Four Rivers i stand
with eyes opened
and outstretched hands
that i may receive
thy blessings Father
anoint me
and
hearken unto my plea
that overflows with the anguish
of illusions endured
and the hunger
for joys still yet desired
that which emanates
within the abysmal depths of me

and i beseech thee
let not death
nor her family of trickery
have its way
nor triumph
this day

for the morrow
when my Sun arises
and recognizes who i am
my sorrow is reconciled
and all vile things
shall no longer be
for i am awakening
and i most assuredly see
the legacy
of the Bliss-filled life
You would have for me
when i commune
and realize
that i am One with Thee

and my Soul Speaks "aye"
and i will not deny
that in a "Twinkling of an Eye"
the lie is vanquished
and the Ancient language of thy love
will be spoken freely once again

we will dance to the tune
and all be it
none too soon
and Truth will forever reign
as my tears rain down
and i submit to the divine acknowledgement
of the presence of the Holy
of all things manifest

i will bask in the light of "BE"ing
seeing
and no longer fleeing
that inner light i could never escape

and i bow in "The Know"
that as the Four Rivers do flow
into Eternity . . . Eternally
that i too am "The Infinite"
and that i am
as i have always been
yes
"I AM"

and in that moment
when the final Epiphany
greets my consciousness
with that Sacred Kiss

i am . . . absolved

Aquarius

i come to you
with the shifting of the Aeon
pouring the Spirit of Life
upon the earth
that you may drink
Water
Life
Consciousness

i bless you

Love is the water of life
for it sustains the eternal Holy,
what you lack
i will suffice

the Thrice Borne greets you
prays to meet you
at the core of your understandings
for the demandings
of your inner child
will not be denied
any more

awaken my children
speaketh the "One"
whom we term Source
and recognize
that you are
as "I" am
One Energy
the ultimate
One Consciousness

i feel your struggle
to live
give me your burden
and like the smoke
of the fat of the Lamb
it shall wisp into the ether

and neither Satan nor Darkness
in their convoluted harkening
can spark a divergence for this course
for i am Source

but a breath away

my life has been my Mecca
the road
the journey
the vision
the purpose

all is the fabric
of one symphonic
orchestrated synonym
of expression

where there is music
i am the lute
for breath
is mine to give
to refute
and i realize my latent harmony

the beauty about me
recognizes my presence
and blossoms
within my conscious awareness
that i may see myself

we dance the jig
Life and i
exchanging leads

i submit to her beckoning
and in my reckoning
she responds
to my sweet soft prayers

understanding
at times eludes my immediacy
but always revisits
for a tease of me
enticing me to
gaze upon her reflection

the pristine waters
with flavors of azure
from the conscious oceans of thought
forms lapping waves
which crests itself
leaving remnants of its visit
in tidal pools
upon the rocky shores
of my desolate beaches
that i may learn the value
of contemplation

and i am ever circumspect

i listen to the syncopated beats
of my pulsing heart
as it keeps perfect time
with the vibratory resonance
of all my experiential-ness
and i begin to implode
in the brilliance within me
likened to that
found in distant multiverses,
a magnanimity that cannot
be contained
nor defined

i hear voices whispering
equations of exponential summations
of unquantified infinities
to which only a God
like you
like me
can answer for ourselves

this is reasonable

is not this the fruit
beyond the concept man embraces
of sweetness
the completeness
that we, man, never seems
able to capture

is this the rapture
we all souls of One Soul expressed
seek
as we journey in wonder
this road to our Mecca ?

and as i meditate
upon the concept
of singularity,
my single eye of reason
becomes an unsheathed arrow
and i become the bow
taught and ready
drawn and directed
to an unspecified target
it is viral in nature

i realize again
a higher calling
for my actualization
and i am loosed

i strike the center of "Now-ness"
and i pierce the illusion of time

i am folding the cloth
the fabric of space
upon itself
and the epiphany
comes
and simultaneously goes
for there is only "NOW"
and that is here, where i must "BE"

a not so ominous truth
it is simple
as am i
but a breath away

so i again
unlock my jaw
part my lips
and divine utterances of joy
copulate with my 'being-ness'
and each moment
becomes an ecstatic shuddering
of orgasmic thoughts
fulfilling its own desires
which were once entombed
in some cloaked memory

but now all stand naked,
exposed
before the mirrored altar
of Source
and in a eternal fleeting glimpse
i see you
i see me
i see all the wisping realities
become a supposition
unto its own presence

and i breathe
and extend my self
with one more step
of an contextual acuity
of assurity
as i meander
towards that city
on the hill
of the holy
which as am i
as are you
but
a breath away

and the parade begins

run feet run ...

wailing
in travail
on every other corner
in the cities
and every steeple
that could be found
pities abound
solemn huh Ma ?

people kneeling
before altars
paying reverent obeisance
in the shadows of crosses
tears flowing . . .
i think

prayers and praises being
shouted
all touting
that phrase
"in remembrance of me"
see Ma . . . i told you
it is time

man finally facing a light
perhaps reckoning
offering sacrifices . . .
what is the meaning
to their hearts ?
i wonder

i ask...
will they suffice
once a year...
even twice
or thrice
still yet denied
denying
could they be lying
while lying those burdens down
only to pick up
where they left off ?

no wonder the tears
queer huh ?

Holy week
a whole week
of torture
carrying crosses
on display
making sure all can see
their burdens on display

is this
for the strong
or the weak ?
i surmise...
with eyes closed

another convenient fairy tale ?
or is this folklore
for the folk
who need it

everybody
is hunting for eggs i think
and that golden goose
they call Jesus
what's the use i ask

me and the drunken ones
sip from our flask again
for the reflection of men
i see
when i look at me
looks good
in a quixotic concussive manner

from this point of inebriation
the psychedelic situational deliberation
it is tolerable now

defibrillate that heart

but tomorrow
when the celebratory times cease
will i again find peace
in the doctrines of my delusional embraces
those jaded systems
of justifications ?

WORD...

i shake my head
cause i know
that God knows
who i am
but i don't like it,

Him seeing me like this

just like i don't like those assholes
that compel me to remember
to turn the other cheek

yeah, turn the other cheek
so they can kiss my . . .

so goes the story
our paths to the glory
carrying burdens of guilt
while our inner lights wilt
before the throne

can you spell "F-O-R-G-I-V-E-N-E-S-S" ?

GOOD FOR YOU !

i should have known you'd see
that when this time of year comes
we all too soon forget
what ills we have let
and still yet
will seek
when this week is over
and out

perhaps that is the blessing
the brevity of man's confessing
sins ? . . . hah . . . amen

and the parade begins
it's Easter again

as i am alone

looking for burdens
i walk the path not alone
to prove the reproof
of my back

give unto me my brother
your hand, your load
and hope will accompany
us to a certain victory
that has already been won

let us speak to the Day's young morn
as the new Sun rises
to kiss our dew laden aspirations

let us break a Holy Bread
that has been prepared
with a yeast of promise

we shall turn the Stone over
that light may bathe
the underside of its hardened stature
and awaken the unseen
into a familiarity
that shant be forgotten
none too soon

with a smile painted
upon the face of our souls
we shall go forward
and give them to the world
as does the wishful sower

who plants a seed
in the garden this day
only to but sit and witness
a coming harvest

yes,
the day soon comes
when that of the vine
has been pressed
and we shall be drunken
as we sit at the table
of the holy offerings of Mother
with a reverent knowing

the children are dancing
as we the elders observe
with a patient tolerable embrace
the blossoming of their hearts

let us not harness their wonder
let us cast expectations to the side
for they serve only to restrain
what may come to be

let us join hands
for the two of us
be joined in a 3rd
and this bond
is not easily broken
as am i . . . not alone

Compellation and Tryst

what innate character within man
compels him to mold such manner
that has him
embrace his muse
with divine affection
in a moment
and thus
turn the shoulder
of conscious rejection

is it the dichotomous aspects
of Soul
the convolution of Spirit and Matter

and it does matter to me
the flatterous words of thee
my muse
as you impart to me
that which i cannot
readily see

and then i shoo you
rebuke you
for you
make my indulgence
of self
uncomfortable
you do
i thought you knew
perhaps you do
as you exact what's due

our appointed times have come
have gone
and at times you come
in rhymes and verse
at times
your words
are terse
as you attempt to disperse
that which is wayward
within

and then
i draw closer
to that mystical place
where i may one day face
my sum

i often contemplate
deliberate
and examine
many such things
as the compellation
and tryst of man

and with your whisperings
i believe i am on to something

i consider just how
does a Muse like you
speak thru
that which confuses me
as you bemuse me
with the breeze from Soul
from heart

but never mind, mind
for mind is being schooled
and ruled
by the illusions
and the delusions it creates
to not suffocate
itself in its own mind stuff
it regurgitates

how does one control a mind
a thought
it's quite easy you see

you take a Truth
and dress it with a Lie
and there belies the quest
of man

or you take a Lie
and veil it with Truth
and man will never understand
and that is but another test

and in my thinking process
i must confess
that i always embraced
Truth as an ultimate
but can i face it,
taste it upon my tongue ?

this is my song being sung

and thus continues
the venue
of the endless seeking
and we believe we are peeking
at the Sun
the Light
held within a Night
but not quite

who was it . . . Descartes
who said
"Cogito Ergo Sum"
"i think therefore i am"
damn him

had we not assumed
would we . . . "BE"

caught betwixt
needing that fix
to become aplomb
and list no more
on the Oceans of consciousness
and find that shore
that safe harbor
where we journey no more
the stormy seas
uttering pleas to the heavens
twixt . . . and
of Compellation and Tryst ?

can you hear that call?

he walked around the landscape of man
with the seat of his pants still dampened
from sitting upon the Dew ladened grasses
of the early morn

yes he still embraced
these magical moments of transformation
as he took a ringside seat
to the new day's glory
on the Skirts of Mother's Garden

he sat in a ambient silence
as he awaited the dawn of this day's symphony
where the fragrance of Mother's offering
danced in the gentle stirring
of life

he could smell the Harvest's fruit
as it whispered its hopes and expectations
to his soul
and he became the exuberant instrument of its song

he cared not about his own appearance
for that which he had witnessed
dwarfed the thoughts of man
and all judgment

all he knew is that
his heart was filled with a light
and he lent this freely
to all who would taste this Joy he possessed
the sweetness he gave

the Gift

he remembers how the Sun of the new day
crept across the landscape in reverence
slowly awakening its Children . . .
and how its vibrant light
touched his naked toes
and warmed them
only to completely envelope him
with an indelible surety
that he was present
and he was

he could still hear the chirping
of those who sat beside him
in this Amphitheater
in the Pews of this Holy Temple
and offered their praise as well
as they commenced with living
and giving back
in songs of joy
and gratitude

yes, he was thankful
each day
for in that stilled moment
within him
he was held by Creation
and the Hand that spawned it all

can you hear that call ?
the Song of your Heart.

at the cross

at the cross
betwixt my compassion
and the realm
of my protective psyche
i am being nailed

my hands have holes in them
and i can neither grasp
nor hold to
any valid logics
nor reason
as to why we are,
so i cling to the etheric qualities
of beliefs
of which are unseen

yes Father, am i forsaken as well
i ask
do tell me
that the crooked paths of life
i have walked
is the right way
and will become straightened
some day

my soles are bleeding
from the spikes of retribution
that have also penetrated my heart
and i leave a trail of blood
evidencing my departure
from that realm
which once embraced my solace
i pray you not take nor follow
my private journey of anguish
nor learn my language
for i know you have your own
to bear
as reason chokes
the light out of its own sanctity

i sit here enveloped
in the folds of time.
we fare well together,
she indifferent
i weary
teary
silently awaiting new fears
to be borne
and manifest unto my here-ness
and each one comes to test my resolve

and "time," she leaves a trail as well
softly etched in the sands of memory
moved by the light winds
laden with wisping values

in my consciousness,
there is a reaching

i am aware
that the effigies
do fade
with each cresting testing wave
that comes to kiss my shores
leaving remnants of other lands
for further examination
and scrutiny
of my mutinous convictions

another juxtaposition
another cross
is visited upon me
that i again may chose
there is no winning nor losing

there is the horizontal plane of "be"ing
and or allowing
and thus the vertical-ness
of ascension
or descension . . .
i smile
my dissension overcomes me

my legs are not broken
and i shall walk on
wandering
in my private wilderness
even with this aching stitch
in my side
from the silly wounds of persecution

and mockery
40 days ?...hah
a cakewalk

my compassion is ever abound
and it does pain me
to see so much woe
within me
about me
within you

in the end
i defend valiantly
most times
the rights of passage
resurrection of the hallowed things brings
e'en if the victory
does appear shallowly hollow

and as i resuscitate,
massage the heart of my inner child
back to life
i tell him the Sun comes soon
and all will be ok
even if at times we do express
and
redress our indifference
with pretty costumes
so none

may assume they know of
our true identity
for this is our lot
to bear this cross
of the lost

yet...
let us be mindful
careful
e'en in our woefulness
to not throw the baby out
with the bathwater
while we offer reverent obeisance
penance and prayer
in our suffering here
bearing the weight of life
at the cross

close our eyes

i close my eyes
in hope that i may not see
my own apathy
and perhaps indifference

but to no avail
for within that singular eye
i hold the vision
of a better life
and something about this,
about me
remains askew
and discordant

i wanted to dance
but i did not hear
the music i desired
so i tried
i vied
and i created my own

delusion ?

i paint pictures every day
of the scenes
of my life
hoping to bring splendid color
but i tire of detail
don't you ?

i draw outside the lines
for conformity
does not fit me well
it is but another girdle
hemming in my girth
my abundance
of my character
yet to be discovered

yes,
life is like that Piano Teacher
yes,
there is music to be learned
to be played
for the entertainment of others
but she, life,
raps my knuckles every time
with its ruler
and i quickly realize the lesson
that she teaches
"You are not in charge!"

of course i rebuke this doctrine
and shouldn't i ?
how would i learn to fly
if i did not leap
from that precipice
to discover such possibilities

we play safe
with loaded guns
roulette they call it

we are rushing,
seeking to die
and be reborn
thus changing reality
yes, it's crazy

the hazy aspects of truth
haunt us all
so we cling
to what eases
appeases
our angst
because we have forgotten
the character
of what is indomitable
within us

in God we have placed our trust
but whose God was He
surely i did not know him
personally
and he has never come
to any of my Birthday Parties

i prayed to this unseen entity
plenty of times
in verse
in lines
in rhymes
and still
i spill my pleadings
hoping for heedings
to my self-created plight
and yet the night endures

where are the cures
for what ails our humanity
our civility
is it our futility
to seek such measures
the treasures of gold
at the end
of our delusory rainbows

who knows
what may come of man

like the Little Choo Choo
I Can, I Can, I Can

it is my rant
my chant
hoping to further convince myself
and us all
that even though we fall
sometimes it is all right
to just lay there and wallow

and when we are finally sick
of our own perspectives
new directives and directions
will appear
on that magical map of soul

so when i consider wholeness
i believe we have all the tools
required
and if not,
being the creators we are
we can fire up the Kilns
and remold our self
into that which we wish
we are pliable are we not

but for me it is the viable i question
which is why
at times
it is so much easier
to just
close our eyes

can you do that for me . . . it only cost a dollar down the street

dollars for crosses at flea markets
jewelry stores and the such
ambiguous self explanatory meanings attached
and perhaps the directions

note :

put cross around your neck
and hang yourself
that you may die
and live again ..

the path to resurrection

not realizing
death is required
that one may be born
again ?
and again . .

i die daily
and i would more often
if i could
it is the only way
to get rid of the poison
that keeps reinfecting my heart

cast the shadows
of dispersion upon me
and give me reason
to take this life
before i take yours

the fleeting pleasures of retribution
offers no solution
to the eternal woes
of my soul

duly noted

you goaded me in to that
causing me to hate your ass

a plausible excuse
but let us go to def-con 3
hear me
and label it reason
another fable
laced with
justifiable insanity perhaps
for this is but
a contextual asylum . . .isn't it ?

inanely put
my chap
said the jester to the rabbit
while mentally masturbating
in Alice's construal dream
who's hole was it ?

the abysmal sickness
were put into the blankets
by those who thought themselves
civilized
calling us savages
go figure
and they bore crosses too

meantime during the age
where sages burned "witches"
with Red Hair ..
they were witches weren't they ?

it doesn't matter
as long as we got the lesson

what lesson you ask

it's simple

grab your cross
and put it around your neck
and voluntarily
give up your life

can you do that for me ?

it only cost a dollar down the street

all is one big Ocean

no, she's not dead
she just went ahead
and i shall meet her at the pass

when i surmise
the time we spent
it went by much too fast

but through it all
the joys we shared
left me with much to tell

and though you still
watch over me
know that i am doing well

see, the love we have
is my hearts salve
and gratitude is my way

and though the winds
of life do blow
in winds we all do sway

but the memories of
our joy-filled love
are memories i shall hold

for in this space
i kiss your face
that smile of shining gold

so make a space
upon your bed
and rose wine i shall bring

as we reunite
man's end in sight
and all the souls shall sing

about the joys
here not deployed
which awaits our final presence

eternity's embrace
all hearts shall taste
the holiest of our essence

the wells shall spring
upon Angel's Wing
and all re-learn to fly

our chains unfettered
no longer tethered
open'd thy single eye

for all is one
under One Sun
the Flower, the Spirit and i

thy soul is cleansed
need not amend
for Soul can not die

so here i stand
need not a plan
for what shall be shall "BE"

and i come to know
as the River does flow
that Life is eternity

all is one big Ocean

created in the image . . . so act like one

i am in pain
it is an indelible poignant suffering
and all the pretty words
offer no buffering
for pain is my truth

since the days of my youth
there has not been
any lasting understanding
to the complexity of bullshit
we endure

for sure,
this damn formula
or experience
you call life
is mostly dark
filled with strife
and the language of anguish
let there be light

who was it that said
life is light ?

if that be true,
then why is there continual contention
amongst us
between me and you
and what are we to do
about it
shit

because of this pain
i have taken my pen
and stabbed my own damn self
in my psychic eye
hoping to relive the jaundice
that accumulates
and expresses
my self-created sarcasms

no dressing it all pretty and shit
changes it

because of my pain
i stab myself daily
without fail
in my sickened heart
that the poisonous blood
of my lethargies
and indifference
and apathy
will not get the best of me
as i bleed
who i want to be
upon the journals
of my tumultuous days
when the light of brotherly love
goes MIA
how you say it ?
Shit . . it hurts

it hurts me to see the smiles of children
and their futures
being attacked
for our lack

of compassion
that has no passion
to sustain itself
always seeking
to explain itself
with reason
and tit for tat
excuses
we blame on our muses
with our contusive thinking process
as we live
under the radar
instead of living
to be our best

this is no damn test
this is the real thing

the wings of thoughts and dreams
it seems
have died
and mankind
who once vied for the greater
became afraid
of their own shadows

and we cower
hoping we will not be discovered
and have to uncover
our apathy
for self
for living

we must begin giving ourselves

spiritual enemas
and get rid of
the lack of our love
and all that shit
that inhibits
our exhibit
of our Cosmic Divine

and no lines
or what lies in between
our inspired verse
can realign us
with our universal purpose

yes i say this

we must step away from the faction
that usurps us from action
and regain our energy
that connects you in me
you and me
me and you
and begin to do
those things
we were created to do
armed to do
for believe it or not
we are all we got
and we are Gods

so act like one

created in the image . . .

but a test you say

the uncertainty of the next footstep
though not prevailing
does have a permanent home
in the recesses of consciousness

with anguish and trepidation
it laces messages of woe unto all
who would listen

we call it wonder
a pretty little term
dressed in pinks and lilacs
to evade our fears

we have already prognosticated the tears
so that failure would not be so stinging
and we then can tell ourselves
"I told you so"
you know what i mean

we have not yet seen
the wonder of our glorious beings
though we dream about it
speak about it
in attempt to conjure it forth
drawing it from the veiled dimensions
of our Supra Consciousness
but those whispering voices
steal our joy

before we can even deploy
something significant
in movement
so we pray
that the day will come
when we are blessed to hit the lottery
or manifest the imagery
of some other far fetched reality
that looms in the silt
buried diamonds
that need to be cleaned and polished
then sold

we sell ourselves short every time
don't we
and yet we beg
plead
to be free
from the Demons we create
that our "Fate"
is understood
and we tell ourselves
we deserve such things

over and over again
we walk this cycle
sometimes we run
that we may again
start all over

funny the pleasure we seek
know that a treasure of self is peeking
as we are seeking
to not discover
the cover of our fears
yet we dare not reveal them
so we seal them
in the seas of our convolutions
again praying for solutions
we already possess

but a test you say
well . . .

Chasing

he was chasing Butterflies
i was chasing Demons
for i wanted to build me a Temple
just like my brother
Solomon

was it wisdom
or the knowing of the names
that gave the ability
to command the legions
ask Issa
he knew
that Solomon knew
the power of word spoken

why do you think we still "Babel" today
what you say ?

this is not token gesture
of info i give to you
just and "in" for
you to understand
that command
comes from the knowing
of how one must be sowing
the spirit of word

Moses spoke
"i conjure"
and that he did
as he spit those words
to alter reality
from a surreality
borne of other dimensions

not to mention
some other lesser shared truths

parting Red Seas to day ?
say, i heard
if i believe
i can . . . achieve
but how does one conceive
or should i say "incieve" ?

let us make a chant
marry it to a vision
and change the world
they did
but i can't
seems to be the order
of our days
our ways
for we cling to illusions
that others create
for our ingestion

suggestion
fall back
listen for God
and call back
or just answer the damn phone
it's ringing
can't you hear it
the Angels singing
"come on home where you belong"

Jacob climbed that ladder
Isaiah and Jeremiah
had visions of grandeur
spawned from the Chariots
of Ezekiel's madness
it is sadness
that we could not have seen
nor learned
how to glean this hull
from our skulls –

duggery is our specialty
as we attempt
to bore our ways to hell
that we may tell
colorful finite stories
of no purpose
but distraction

like the roller coaster ride
at the Disney Land of attraction
we are attracted to the
Dizzy lands
where in the cosmic theme
nothing is eternal
nor seems
aright

our sight is fixed
never aplomb
save when we delude our selves
as our collective senses
collude to the allusions
baited in our schizophrenic
examinations of things

let me have ½ dozen Blue
and Mac,
you better give me the other ½ dozen
Red
yeah, those pills for ills
so i can be balanced
in my vacillations
'twixt Truth and whatever

forever i was hoping
but in the end
are we really coping
with anything lasting

perhaps the Saints
were fasting
for a reason
i don't know
i would just like life
to flow
without a hitch
that bitch

my her lips are pretty
and the allure
for sure
is enticing
and the sufficing
i accept
all the while
chasing Demons
while you chase Butterflies

but i'm not sure it's poetic

many poets write about poetry
and then
a few write from an objective
point of view
about the writing of those poets
who write about poetry

a sort of subjective / objective
quandary

this is a very semi-disconnected
examination of inanity
an insanity
that only a poet
can understand

for what is semi – disconnected

like being ½ a virgin

only a poet can be a virgin
and a whore
simultaneously

objectively speaking of course

now that's being subjective
i think

but i'm not sure it's poetic

Cogito Ergo Sum

Epiphanic convolutions
devoid of solutions
grip my soul
with a scurrilous embrace
in a life-death struggle
of co-dependency

my tribulations
continue the march
forward / backward
cloaked in a dark veil
for i just cannot let go
of that which i have been fed

whether it be Christian Sciences
or other compliances
or indoctrinated propaganda
matters not much these days
for the relevance to all
that i think i know
exceeds not this empirical containment

we have labeled such misnomers
with pretty little collections
of letters
as we attach semi-cosigned
significance and values

for a determined outcome
that can project
and chart the movement
of the people
and thus the Souls
Faith, Trust, Belief
are quantified
with intangibles
and an etheric fabric
called the unseen

my soul does in fact
recognize itself
in this wisping curtain
of abysmal nothingness
or it created
such a reflection
for we do vie
for valuation
at some point
don't we

but in the nearby end
of things
our champion of spiritual indifference
remains but a few unresolved
age old questions
such as . . .
why
and
what if

and hearing not any
verifiable retorts
we resort
to impersonal validations
for "Self" begs for reflection
that errs not
through time

and through the dark, the light
the dawning, the night
we are left
with but one possible truth
which Descartes
so aptly coined
and that simply is
"Cogito Ergo Sum"..
i think therefore i am . . .

Chaos

there is a presence
a chaotic noise
awaiting its turn to speak
lurking in the shadows
on the fringes of my peace
seeking naught but opportunity
to poison and infect my consciousness

yes, these voices
they offer reason
laced with a twisted logic
that we all can understand
and relate to
but you
can never get rid of them
once they move in

they look to sleep on your bed
lay their head
beside you
on your soft pillow
that they may whisper
in moving silent syllables
to you
in your ear
in lieu
of dreams of beauty
and other sweet ecstatic things
so we think

and we awaken
each morning
carrying forth
the darkness of doubt
into a world of sunshine
and rising suns
giving them to our Sons
and our Daughters
drawing no quarters
as we diligently attempt
to slay their futures
labeling life with such things
as respect
and obedience

i call it forced acquiescence

we make careful incisions
and infect their open wounds
that fester in their eternal souls
we pretend to suture
the holes
with the offerings
of empty
meaningless
and false compassions

but why do we have
such passions for darkness
and self-inflicted pain
found under the rock of rote
and rite
and doctrine
and dogma

can you build a house upon it
shit
i think not

for it is a rock
that rocks
and sways
each day
with the winds of change
and challenges
for it is a house
that stands on its own
only in the enigmatic imaginings
of mad men
and women too
like me
like you

within each of us
there is chaos
to which we apply
such rationalizations
of actualizations
with validations
and falsely induced
affirmations

we feed this to our offspring
that they may grow to be like us
and we see that same bullshit
in the reflections
of their characters
looking just like us

i am not impressed

have we ever
truly addressed the truth
that we know Jack Shit
yeah he lives next door
a doctrinal whore
who sells her soiled panties
to all who would listen
polished and glistening
the lies
to make them a bit more palatable

but a mistruth
fib
fable
deliberate misinformation
or whatever we wish to call it
is still a lie
so let us clear the table
and start all over again

clean the pots Ma
scrub them well
let us loose
all remnants of Hell
before we prepare the meal
we are all too willing to eat
and feed our children

let us not give this present
from the presence
to the world to come
by accepting the redundancy

of stupidity
and insensitivity
and indifference
with deference
and an alacrity
of our own numbness

let us sit in the silence
and take watch
and observe
the shadows dance for attention

move not
close you ears
to the incessant whispering
of their reason
and logic
for what comes thereafter
are the lost souls
who continue
the venue
and there
is but chaos

again . . . i've been here before

in my Father's house
there are many mansions
each one has one
won't you open the door
and invite me in
neighbor

let us sit by the fire
and commune with the presence
do not you and i make 3?

you see, the words not heard
seemingly matter not
for we have heard them before
we just somehow forgot
that our songs
are the Holy Grail of truth

let us sup some wine
and inebriate ourselves
and become drunken with love

and barriers of confusions
which manifest contusions
of our spirit
will chaff and fall away
and then perhaps
we will re-experience

the rippling
and co-centricities
in our little ponds
of perception
in a while all vile things
will be remembered no more
and i will offer you my cheek
for a kiss
and my hand
that i may grasp yours
and draw you to "Self"
for that sweet brotherly embrace
found in union

we will lose ourselves
in the dance of pixies
of muses
of butterflies and angels
and Father will smile
within the abode
of our hearts

what say you
may i visit my goodness
upon the threshold
of thine own

i am disrobing myself
that i may stand true
stand naked
and in the way of light
at the Altar of Creation

won't you allow me in
that we may sit and commune
i with thee
with i
again ?

i am no stranger
i have been here before

a parent's tears.. a parent's fears

the anger and indignation aside
i cannot hide
from this anguish
i must bear

and no matter the volume of tears
the volume of my love
can never again be fulfilled
for my son
was killed

i think, i think, i think
this can not be true
can it ?

a night mare
of hurt

i go to his room
expecting him to be there
playing video games
or sleeping
and he is not

oh i have not forgotten him
the walls remind me
for they are weeping too
for him
for me
for you

his bed is as he left it

shit !

Sneakers tossed about
i remember when i gave him the money
i said to him "honey isn't that a bit much"
his hand touched mine
as i cosigned
to his dreams

it seems
like that was our last time

i remember the smile on his face
i could taste his joy
and pleasure
in my heart

that smile
is one of my cherished treasures
as are so many others

i carried him
for 9 months
waiting
anticipating
seeing his face
and now
i never will again
for now i have only pictures
and memories
and my anger
but that will not make him come home

my thoughts roam aimlessly

without cease
and there is no peace within me
to be found

all i see is my son
laying face down
in the ground
dead
that picture
will never leave my head
nor my spirit

his final words
i can hear it
playing over and over
his call
"Mommy"
dammit
this shit hurts
it hurts
my Son is gone
and each day since
the dawn i have cursed

Lorde why
why
did my son have to die
this way
any way
any day

i look at his father
and i see Trayvon
i look at any son

and i see Trayvon
i close my eyes
and i see
Trayvon

he may be gone for you
but for me
he and i are bonded
connected
forever

the tears as a parent
offers no relief
for the belief of this travesty
is so surreal

people eulogize
express their hate
anger
sympathy
and empathy
when all i want God
is to see Trayvon
walk into this room
and remove this cloak of gloom
that has moved into my life
because of that night
when my son
died
and took my life's Sun
away

a parent's tears .. a parent's fears

born on the Fourth of July

2 days before her birthday
she gained her independence

yes, she was liberated
from having to carry a body around
her Soul was set free
from the toils
and the snare
the worries
and the cares
that life often affords one
here

many people were not too happy
about the idea
of her crossing over
but our anger
and our grief
offered no respite
no relief
and even we
abandoned our beliefs
that she was going
to a better place

how could we face
life without her?

well i guess we will continue
to find out
with out a doubt
we will have to somehow
make it through
cause she was through
fighting through
this life
the strife
the rife
on 2 July 2006

you see
she was an Independence Baby

born on the Fourth of July

R.I.P. Virisa A. Cohen – Peters
4 July 1957 ~ 2 July 2006

again today

o where o where
o where is my mask
which one should i wear this day
my dear my dear
let me hide my face
before i go out to play

the tears i shed are hidden inside
i don my mask that i may hide
and perhaps i can fool myself as well
but i can't, i can't i tried

so when the play is over
our true faces must be uncovered

but just the same

o where o where
o where is my mask
which one should i wear this day
my dear my dear
let me hide my face
before i go out to play

again today

but the letting go

the perdulous children
were in need of a place
to rest their weary souls

the journey
from here to eternity
has been an arduous trek
and they have yet to arrive
in the "Now"

sunshine avoided their way
like a plague
for they have been ostracized
from the realm of men's acceptance
for they dressed their countenance
with a different light

there was no anguish borne
that could embrace their convictions
they counted all things joy
and joy it was
for lessons
were littered everywhere
and they were the students
who have come to impart
to those who would listen
a means to pierce Illusion's veil

the dichotomous aspects of existence
they knew all too well

for without Joy
what purpose would pain serve

it is through pain
that seeds may shed their hull
sprout
crest the furrow
blossom
and hopefully
some day bear
a fulfilling edible fruitful delicacy
that liberates man
from his self-induced bondage
that which we all secretly vie for
have died for
so many times
over and over again

these children were the emissaries
of something beyond the absorption
of our reason

so we rejected the possibilities
that we not be disturbed

we would rather
be perturbed with them
for the shaking of the bridge
that connects us to something
beyond the grandness
of this mess
we have and choose
to endure

yet the door remains ajar
for in truth
it cannot be closed
and the light remains vigilant
though we do not the same

there are names
etched upon the walls of our souls
that have not been spoken
since that Christed One
"parabalized" in code the wonder
that liberated us from the anchors
which keep us submerged
in the Sea of forgetfulness
as we slowly drown

we claim we want to swim
and thus fly
remembering such things
as wings
we once adorned
so many aeons ago

can you feel the wisping ghosts
who whisper in your ear
telling through your verse
that they still live
to but liberate you
from your self-enslavement
i do

the Flowers and Butterflies
are but deliberate metaphors
that are strategically placed
in your journey
as are smiles

they are placed to perhaps
provide a spark
that may ignite
that torch you carry
inscribed with a
"woe is me" credo
you have ascribed to
without question

but what is the question
you would pose to God?
another "Why"
and i ask why

why do we ask of things
for which we are the answer
the power
to alter
the way we should go
let us not falter
any longer
let us remember
that we are the children
of the Source Prime
and that which has abandoned us
was never really worth having

and if we are the children
who have been cast away
from a formed world
of a dumbed down
numbed down
dense expression of life
we should as James did speak
count it all joy
for there is nothing for us to deploy here
but the letting go

and i ask

and i ask
are we but stewards
of this decaying vessel?
and to what end
do we inhabit
such a place

and i ask
or are we passengers
on this "Life" ride
looking out the portals
hoping for glimpses
of some certainty
some contextual reality
that is not fleeting
as we are seeking
an understanding
while vacillating
between the beggings
the demandings
of disclosure
of the destination
that we may look forward
to closure
as life streaks by
on the fly
towards the unknown
other worlds . . .

and i ask
the seeds we have sown
will we see the harvest
will we taste the fruit
will we see the smiles
upon the faces of others
our children
or look in the mirrors
and be blinded by the smiles of our own

and i ask . . .
as our sisters and brothers
taste the offerings we have submitted
to the essence of this experience
we have nurtured
with our worries
our doubts
our bouts with the demons
of our own making
our fears
our blood
our sweat
our tears
and our laughter

and i ask
where is this land
where resides
the "Happy Here After"
is it fable
or Myth
or Lies
or Lore

just the same
i do want more
don't you ?

and i ask
Who or What
is that One
who can provide the solutions
and ultimate resolutions
to the Broken-ness of man

and i ask . . .
what have we done
to deserve this end
of chasing the reconciliatory ether
where neither
i nor you
have a valid clue
on where our next step
serves the greater
and not the continuing venue
of questions
and empty suggestions
for our ingestions
and temporary still-ness of tongue
so i ask

and i ask

and that i am

i have died a million times
at least
but who was counting
the countless breaths
where life with its frailties
hung
suspended
by hopeful unconscious tethers
to the offerings
of Flora
and her family of verdant embrace

my exigent pleadings
for but another feeding
were met without contest
yet with a humble offering
she enticed me
to take my fill
and that i did

i watch as the
alchemy of her presence
of essence within
transformed
the most obscure
regions of my inner being
to shed their cloaks
and partake in the bounty
of the dance
as life celebrates itself
in such reflective grandeur

and i smile
for i know that i too
now give back
with every expression
every expectoration
every exhalation
and Floras' Children
are fed by the same mindlessness
with an automation
that needs not be held in scrutiny
but that of a reverence
embraced by continual gratefulness
for life

and that i am

this is why i sleep . . .

i want to have sex with my dreams

i want to impregnate them

with not possibility

but a certain verifiable probability

that will bear a flock of children

all named "Reality"

this is why i sleep . . .

Vision Quest

There is a vision in my Soul, and i call it home.
It is that which completes me.

I can feel my toes in the soil,
bringing forth instant recognition
which transcends the passage of the eons
i have been away from my true love . . . Home.

She welcomes me in all her regality,
kissing my cheeks with the warmth of her love
the sunshine of her smile
caressing my brow

She beckons me into her chamber
and there is a table
filled with the divine fruits
from her garden of love
where her own sweat lovingly
nourished each and every seed

my seat at the table's head
sits empty, waiting for me,
calling my name.

We speak beautiful things

We speak beautiful things
Telling ourselves it is our Soul-Speak
Yet we live ugly
Detesting the divine
As we detest "self"
And all its shortcomings
Perceivable failures

Failing is not an option
To those who seek the lesson
Confessing that we are weak
When we are strong
Is a direct affront
On our greater selves

us for Breakfast

it was a day like any other day
or so it seemed
heart was beating
with no direct input from me
Thank God
for i would most certainly screw it up
or forget to keep my mind to task
if i had to be responsible

The chest was still grabbing that air
systematically
except when i intervened
to draw on my cigarette

i went outside
like i do every morning
to offer my obeisance, prayer and gratitude
for just being here

i looked about me
the trees were still . . . . trees
standing rooted in the earth about me
still swaying to a light wind
while reaching for the heavens

was i emulating them,
or they mocking me ?

the sky was a very light blue
the Sun was what the Sun was
slightly warm, slightly yellow
all light

but...
it appeared to be in a different place
than yesterday at this time

i pondered this
and minds liked that
early morning thoughts to play with

and then the variety of considerations came
and the game of possibilities began

just suppose the Sun is really moved
but 15 degrees to the north ?
or was it Mother who has shifted ?
what would happen

would the Earth open up
and swallow us for breakfast
from Kosovo to Texas
from England to Japan
funny
the powerlessness of man

i wondered then
where does all these thoughts go ?
are they being stored someplace ?
a place where i would meet them again
Lorde knows there are many i would like to forget
have them wiped from my memory
for i am not anxious to know
that they too are eternally mine

these thoughts...
will they ever complete themselves

be reconciled
unto their own path
or are they destined to wander
waiting in some suspect position
to ambush me again
mug me again
to encounter and struggle
like Jacob?

break my Thigh Divine Angel
and then redeem me
rename me
let me become a nation

they were meant to be lost
not for me to re-find
that junk
and disdain
and pain
and nonsense
that once made sense
in my sickened mind
you know what i mean
yes, the mean stuff
like
indifference
hate
towards self
and others

i think i forgave myself
but i do still faintly remember
some incidences
and the defenses

of my less than valiant character

funny
how the thought of being perished
brings upon us
these not so cherished moments
yet we hold on to them
in memory of our almost dead pasts
that lasts
and lasts
and lasts
always casting shadows
into our presence
a gift
a contribution of sorts
to our Karma i guess

a test perhaps ?

sometimes i think this but a school
you know ... life
and fools like me never get it
or do we ?
and just do not confront
those items
we hide in the back of our closets
along with that child we once knew

Viktor Frankl spoke
of our existentialism
and the schisms betwixt self
and reality
me ...
i got plenty of them

i thought it was my job to create them
isn't that what dreaming is for
to escape who we are
to go in our proverbial kitchens
and bake cakes
with pretty colorful icings
so that we can like the bowls
of our bowels of reason clean
and pretend we are desert
for the world about us

which ushers fort another concern
before i burn
so they tell me
and that is trust
TRUST?
why is it always the unseen?

that being the situation
we all can believe in whatever we choose
couldn't we
but in the end
i do not think it would stop
the Earth from swallowing
us for Breakfast
do you?

after all...
do not we eat our young?

who am i

who am i
that life would deem me worthy
worthy of persecution
and crucify me

who am i
that my own brothers
should turn their face from me
deny me
and fear to look upon my brightness

who am i
that men should forever keep
my name upon their lips
speaking undue praises
or dispersions

who am i
that life offers unto my soul
no assistance
that i may find my own way
by way of my own inner light

who am i
that my eyes
see but transient evil
as it comes to discern
the Holy in all things

who am i
that the essence of life
the breath of the divine
be mine to enjoy
employ
deploy
all the days
of my journey here

who am i
that this Cosmic Symphony
plays privately
for me
for you
to enhance the consciousness
of our hearts
and give unto us song
that we may dance

who am i
that the children
indulge me
with their innocence
their smiles
and their trust

who am i
i that dreams freely
as i choose
as i walk the path
of my own visions
and my own righteousness

who am i
that comes to know
this ever expanding realm
of the possibilities
of what "Love Is"
and can do,
that love that embraces me
feeds and nourishes me
with a certain sovereign goodness
that i may taste
the sweet fruits
of life's daily harvests

who am i
who am i
that you would consider
the "i" in me
in thee

who am i

Today i lost my faith

i look around at this world
my world
and i see suffering
yet there is hope
i see Hunger and Famine
and they tell me to just pray
i see Brothers of the same Father
killing their Divine Family Members
and they tell me to hold on to my Faith
well, today i lost my Faith

Is it my Faith that will make a change
as i get down on my Knees to pray to something unseen
and perhaps not known
i do know that there is something greater
i feel it within the core of who i am
but how, just how do i activate this power?
this hour, this minute, right now

many will tell you that we have the power within
that we must move away from our sin
me, i just wish to awaken
from this nightmare we call life
to move away from the strife
and into a reality of permanence
laced with Joy
embraced by all
who hears this call
for change
Today i lost my faith

The old ways do not seem to work
for me
you see
there is no certainty
that the veil will be removed
that the Sail of our Ships of Hope
shall gather a wind
that takes us to that promised land
perhaps it is i who does not understand
but with all due certainty
we will all die
some day . . . some how
Today i lost my faith

i have laid down my life of old
many times before
as i examine the soul of who i am
in theses feeble rhymes
from the heart of a man
a Hued-man
and still i stand here
with my color and song
singing hymns of praise and joy
my life long

and still yet the relief i seek
may be here with me this week
but next week it comes late
it has vacated the everlasting
while the saints have been fasting
for a million years
and all the tears of us ordinary people
who have acquiesced to being the sheeple
of something perhaps still yet unknown

have i not my garden kept
even while my anguish has slept
at some time we all have wept
have not my seeds of hope been sown
Today i lost my faith

i spoke with a friend
about this very same situation
there was nothing uplifting
to that elevation with elation we sought
or have been taught
and i bought it
until now
in my vexation
Today i lost my faith

they say life is a present
but at times i must question
who wrapped this gift
for it seems
that all the goodness
can only be embodied in dreams
so as we drift once again to sleep
there is a despair type symphony
and i hear your soul weep
for what it once had
remembered
from January to December
and back again
Today i lost my faith

don't get me wrong
it is Faith that changes the tune of this song
i hear through my doubts and my fear
and many a tear
has been shed
upon the pillow on my bed
and where is this Bridegroom of Spirit
that i must wed
if it is within
then let us bring it on my friend
why the shyness of spirit
i know you are there
for the drum beat, i hear it
i march daily
attempting to attune my "Self" with "i" Self
to some ethereal avail
and the children of Source continue to wail
the children who have embodied such things as
greed, war, child prostitution
in this convoluted institution
the children of slavery
i will behave

just pray they say
have faith in the seen and the unseen
well i am tired of being blind
i wish to leave all this shit behind
i wish to clear this vexed mind
and that of my brothers and sisters too
you know what i mean
i need to touch, taste, smell and fully sense

without recompense
this mean unseen love for me
that keeps playing this game of hide and seek
am i not being diligent
Today i lost my faith

what i do know that is without my faith
this stuff is somewhat unbearable
and we realize our fears
the same ones who have been sitting
on the other side of our consciousness
all these years
as i walk this path
taking an inventory for all i have
have had
yes i am somewhat glad and thankful
for i do hold the visions in my eyes
of something greater to come
and i recognize
that our sum
is much greater than the collective
and from one soul to another
this is not selective
nor discriminatory
for the story is not about our differences
but of our similarities
without disparity
and with an absolute clarity

we must embrace each other
without reservation
nation to nation
culture to culture
gender to gender
from abundance to nothingness
from indifference to deference
if we are to change this mess
and if this is but a test
we must pass
together
as one
to get this done
and though Today i lost my faith
i have found my Power
and that is my Love . . .
for you

Today i lost my faith

we believed

a dimension apart
a world never capable
of being imagined
where all is surreal

miracles litter the way
and the middle eye
is one of manifestation
and all thoughts actualize

Alice knew not of this place
and Dorothy could not face it
and i long to taste it
as do all souls
once again

such things
as warmth and cold
right and wrong
exist not,
and we forgot
what the absence of time feels like
haven't we

in our now fantasy
we see through
kaleidoscopic glasses,
nothing is clearly defined
so we refine the illusions
with loosely gathered allusions

minds askew from reality
whatever that may be,
and what do we truly believe
at our prime level,
do we really understand
how to revel in joy ?
"we" branded rebels of the realm

at the helm of our consciousness
which i term my private asylum
there is a madman
standing in judgment
of things that do not matter

like the mad hatter
we pacify ourselves
with the changing of the costumes
or the parts thereof
whereof
we remain lost
tossed in the void
where we dream of a substance
we term life
which exists not
at any sustainable
measurable
accountable
endurable
capacity,
where the insidious
become a ridiculous

a fleeting validity
in our conformity
to the programs
that are running in our heads

and here in this limited
timid
insipid
exposure to self

we feel justified
vindicated
because we have learned
how to manipulate the delusion
coming to an inane conclusion
that we are OK . . .
sometimes

we embrace ourselves in love
from the left hand
as self-condemnation and purgatory
are ushered forth
from the right-mindedness
of our needs
viscerally so

and when i attempt to ask the question
"what do i know"
Truth is
if i can call it that
it is like the fat

of the Sacrificial Lamb,
up in smoke
just like David said it would be
in some Psalm or another

and my Mother
she never warned me about this

i kiss the bliss i never quite had
just like my Father, my Dad
who too yearned
to make a way
through this wilderness . . .
bless Him
bless them

and the quest continues
consciousness'
and contextual fabrics
of my reality
being shredded
in my reflective examinations

the damnation of overt scrutiny
offers no solace
but for a blink of that eye
which is infected,
a less than Divine Stye
blurring all perceptions
when i ponder eternity
and certainly with age

it gets no better
save when i lie
to self again

i hear the Dogs barking
would that be some sort of alarm
that the Thief has entered the gate ?

and men with undeterminable Egos
run to get their Capes
laced with a scent of fear
and their Egoic need to show the world
we have some courage
to transform the norm
of our little selves
into Gods

i laugh at this juncture
for the tincture of truth
still burns the wound
profusely
as i contusivley observe
in my concussive state,
my own alacrity for stupidity
"Oh Quixotic One when will you get the lesson?"

so . . .
i grab my gun
loaded with subterfuge
and the deluge of reason begins
and in conclusion

i resolve this . . .
thou art my enemy,
my friend,

and the dichotomous ghost
awakens once more
and haunts my weary
tear-laden soul
but i worry not
for the hole in my heart
does serve its purpose
alleviating the angst
i once so dearly cared about

i could simply say . .
"i don't give a fuck",
but that would be a confession
even my indifferent self
cannot bare in the open,
the light
that transcends opposites
in my behavior

Man . . .i am still stuck
looking for a Savior

so i shout silently
that i not disturb your solemn rest
lest you are ready
for if we do chose to awaken
we must voluntarily
summarily

spit upon the buried coffin
of who we used to be
or who you think
you may have been
for the many eons
we have slumbered
resting in an uncertain peace

and who was it that said
"the Least shall lead a nation"?

and to my reasonable elation
i am cool with that
for it does appease some aspect
of this itch for
what lies beyond the door
of the horizons
we peer at
leer at
from our spat upon graves

and i with an abundance of exuberance
i wave
cheering, jeering
"Heeeeyyyy . . . HOOOOOO"

behave the Voice said !

was that in my head alone
or did you hear the echo as well
of your own voice
reverberating
in the empty halls ?

Halls … Walls … empty
save for pictures and visions
of fading dreams

and as much as i deliberate
about the sheer ecstasy
of total liberation
there still resides my anguish
and i ultimately surmise
but one thing
and this may be
why the Caged Bird does sing
at times

and that is …
the sin of it all
we heard that call
and we answered …

we believed … didn't we

the Perfect People Pledge

i being of sound mind in my own mind, being perfect do hereby solemnly pledge this oath of my transient truth that i, (fill in name) being perfect do have the right to judge others, condemn those who do not meet up to my vacillating standards.

i being as perfect as i am do acknowledge that any reflective apparatus i use to look at my self whether it be introspection of a mirrored reflection are but tools that i may build my own self esteem and thereby see others, my brothers and my sisters as less than me.

i being perfect, hold to my inalienable assiduous right to point fingers at others and to perform without reservation the following tasks . . .persecution, gossip, lie, cheat, steal, snicker, make fun of, and any other acts that i may deem justifies my superiority as a human whatever.

won't you climb with me

i exuberantly embrace
the toils of my day
as i make yet another arduous climb
of this mountain
which stands before me

i but hope to ascend
and sit upon its peak once again
hoping to grasp a peek
at a passing muse or two

bring to me a verse
bring to me a word
that entices the clouds
to undress their wonder
and stand before my throne naked
that i may see clearly
the once held mysteries
heaven has veiled from me
and my empirical nature

the wind ushers forth my Terpsichore
whose perfectly syncopated choreography
speaks to my soul
in a tango like shuffle
awakening a divine reason
that only when i in-spire
can be translated to paper

my pen is my rapier
and it cleaves me
from my "Self"

and the reasonable values i held
but a moment ago

they becomes as dust
a countless thing
that will cloud one's earthly eyes
with anguish
and confusion
and a lost melancholy
that teases our need
to become an unsatiated prevalence

look from thy inner eye brother
and the sound will manifest
in to a syllabic courtship
with your soul
speaking in alchemic tones
as you vibrate
and resonate
a strange bereft music
that can only be expectorated
from your prodigious being,
your unquantifiable regality
a sovereignty
that is foreign
to our way

but this can only be experienced
upon the mountain
come my friend . . .

won't you climb with me

Dedicated to Myiya Imani Rai

they are people . . . too

there are many people
who will never have anything
to say to you
but much to say about you

they are people . . . too

there are many people
who watch what you do
waiting in the bushes
to ambush you
about the road you choose

they are people . . . too

there will be many people
who like what you do
but cannot say this to you
for they do envy you
and all you do

they are people . . . too

there are many people
who thrive
to incite the sheeple
to tear down your steeple
even as you are building it
shit

they are people . . . too

there are many people
who offer you love
and some do want more than this
from you . . .
be careful whom you enlist
to enjoin you vision
you bliss

they are people . . . too

and then . . .

there are people
who are just a blessing,
there when your soul
is being tested
in your trials
your tribulations
your deliberations
about life
and yes
thank God

they are people . . . too

there are people
who offer you solace
and rest
and peace
without cease

they embrace you
kiss the face of you
and your dreams . . .
and again
i thank God
for these people
and you know it

they are people . . . too

there are many types of people
the naysayers
the way layers
the surveyors
evaluating you
and all you do

some who applaud
and laud you
and what you do
some are the frauds about you
there are some who condemn
never realizing
in their surmising
they but condemn themselves
i pray for them
for . . .

they are people . . . too

The World that is becoming Real

in a world
where we walk in our sleep
we look on with indifference
as the children do weep
promises are made
we intend not to keep
we live in the shallows
while lost in the deep

we profess to seek truth
while embracing the lie
pretending to live
while each day we die
we paint on a smile
while inside we cry
accepting illusions
and never ask why

looking to heavens
for forgiveness of sin
delusions abound
created within
transfigurative salvation
by Genie or Jin
the pathways of losers
dreaming to win

our dance and our laughter
laced with travail
upon stormy seas
less rudder less sail
dis-ease with our brethren
undiagnosed ail
yet i hear souls crying
with silent night wail

but hold to your hope
for the sun soon come
in light of the new day
we realize our sum
the pathway revealed
to whence we are from
and spirits attuned
all minds now aplomb

and joy in the streets
of Gold we will dance
for all "Is" is perfect
'twas never with chance
each touch of our love
perpetuates advance
i'll see you at the party
and we'll sing perchance

in the world that is coming to be

you are 2 dammmmmed

you are 2 dammmmmed
phaseeshus
that is wat she tole me

it was a fishious psyckle
that neva seamed to nd

we wur all deelooshunall
i thunk
but wat cood i say
perhaps i shood sing
or sang
that poetic nashunal antler

you know it
don't u

Oh say can u sea

i need a mintaur

help

Tomorrow Perhaps

i was walking down the street
where 1,000 gallons of Petrol
is burned every second

people sauntering, commingling
attempting to fill and occupy their lives
with something
anything
like
conversations
interactions
discoveries
and new encounters
yet the day is the same
as the one before
and perhaps
the one to come

some of us have forgotten
the sum of who we are

does any one care about the portrait
the painter
the frame
the canvass
with living vivid colors ?

a man walked up to me
made a common city gesture
putting his slightly spread
index and middle fingers
to his lips...
no, he was not blowing me a kiss

but this is what i thought
that he was asking for a cigarette
yet, all he wanted
was a light

all right... alright
my fear and my tightly bound selfishness
reacted
for that simple 2 fingered action
spawned my reaction,
for this enactment of process
had become my truth...
but all he wanted was a light

as i turned the corner on Broadway
life abundant met me
my vision
my consciousness
in a broad way
who could possibly sleep through this
yet still
so many were
sleepwalking
talking to each other
and to themselves

stuck in their dreams
and dreamless days
their ways of coping
some hoping
that the self-doping would alleviate
them from being lost
and delegate to them a path
many not . . . perhaps

and perhaps the voices we hear
i hear
may be laced with fear
and doubts
and bouts with self

but i suspect, i doubt
that life is simplistically more complex

in the bowels of my own vexations
i saw nor felt the liberation
i vie for
and though i may say "Die For"
i am living for
an opportunity
to cry for help
yelping like a dog inside
from the place i hide

i too am a vagrant wanderer
clawing, holding on
to the visceral strings of my wonder
playing tunes
along with my self-created
orchestrated

symphonies

so while something spiritual in me
resonates with what was about me
the ambiance embraced me
and began to speak to me
loudly
and
now i too want to hold on

i pulled out my camera
and began to take pictures
of the busy-ness
to make the assist
in my endeavor to record
the accord
of life

i wonder do they see me
as the oddity
the oddity of a color unique
within this creative expressive painting
of one portrait of life
i see them . . . i see me

there were the vendors of the streets
the lenders quite replete
all giving, offering an option
to barter away their prizes
for yours
and of course
many took the bait

and though some may appear to be
in disdain
at the fleeting joys
the enduring pain
and all the inane, insane
twain the two
i see life evolving
devolving
unto itself
while we are attempting
the solving of equations
to the situations
we encounter
or not

some are dormant and waiting for sunshine
some shedding their hulls
to rise above the furrows
and perhaps it may not come today
but there is always
tomorrow . . . perhaps

well...

i was in my Sock Drawer digging
looking through my underwear drawer as well
in the closet
under the bed
i bumped my head
for...
i was looking for a delusion
that would fit this day
i needed one badly

the way was dark
and i needed some light
even if it was but an illusion
created for my sedated self

i woke up this morning tired
grateful yes, for i did awake
to what ? is the issue

the same old perspectives greeted me
in the form of Emails
and messages
and posts
and i knew right then
that the first 3 hours of my day
was toasted
a waste ?

yes i needed a delusion
that would fit this contusion
where my heart was bruised yesterday
and the day before
as it is every day

the score is
Home ~0~
Visitors ~0~
and my Hero is still
the Silver Surfer
what for you ask ?
'cause he can escape
with no need of a cape
like Superman
or Batman
or that man
who feeds me lies
every day
that he knows the way
is the Truth and the Light

where is it i ask
what is the task
of obeisance i must perform
is it prayer
the loosing of my fear
or is more tears raining down on my Soul
that is required ?

the Fire is not out
but i am pissed
to be constantly dismissed
to gather more damn wood
shit i have clear cut the forest already
and Betty and Boo
still give me the finger
and in other words or gesture
they say "F" you too
what are we to do . . . now

some how i must find that perfectly fitted delusion
that fits like a glove
they keep telling me
it is love
well . . .

yet we shine

the valiant quest of Perseus
has not gone unnoticed
by the Gods

sword drawn in victory
brandishing the head
of Medusa

for his prize
he was given a Galaxy
of wonder
we now call Andromeda
whose beauty they claimed
exceeded that of Nereids
but who stood in judgment

the contemplative aspects of man's quest
to become inscribed
in the annals of time
as His Story of sorts
contorts our reason
as we resort to such antics
with our frantic
logic loosed movements

the Zeus' of our world
herald in new edicts
confounding our good intent
but good intent
serves no master
save that of reward

in the end
the Persephone
win always
and the Queens
do relinquish their realms
and perhaps sovereignty
to another Cassiopeia
who waits in the folds
of time yet to arrive
into our Now-ness

and what is the "Myth"
of the 12 Olympians
will there ever be a clarity
that allows us to
see the light of
each Star's Soul

yet we shine
embolded
enfolded
in a flux
with a crux
to bear new tale

yet we shine

They would have a King

and the Lorde said unto Samuel . . . "it is not thee that thy children reject, but it is I. It is I who brought them out of Egypt and through the desert, yet still they worship all else."

>we squander our life
>as we wander
>with wonder
>through our desolations
>
>the sands of the deserts
>of our barren lives
>rise to greet us
>to parch the lips of our Souls
>and bring forth our thirsts
>that can not be quenched
>yet we drink not
>
>we erect Temples of Madness
>with idols who have no power
>and we come to love them
>their falsehoods
>instead of the Source
>of our Gifts
>the Hand that made us all
>
>our proverbial Moses
>bade us to listen
>but the noise
>and subterfuge
>of our lives
>and our short lived jovialities
>drowns out the whispers of truth,
>yet she whispers still

to those who hunger
for the spirit
of word actualized

and the children dance
intoxicated
by their own delusions
their self-created Hell
for which they beckon
my unstilled grace
for salvation
from the Demons
they have invited
into their homes
now rendered
but a house

a house of ill repute
whose roof
can not stop the rains
of their anguish

they pray for One
who would lead them
through their endless landscapes
and their wilderness'
filled with their own misery
but they listen not
to their own hearts
that they may discern
the Fair Way of Love

Nay,
they travel the road
of a living perdition
content to embrace
dreams of that madness
that has infected their consciousness
with an incurable want
a incessant desire for "Things"
which can never be satiated

Yes,
my children want a leader
a King
someone to save them
from their woes
and one whom they can blame
when these very same woes
revisit their abodes
and sit at their tables
and spoil the meal
and lay ruin
to the mirth
their misguided lives
embrace in their
askewed perspectives

Yes,
i shall answer their prayers
in My Own Way
My Own Time

and i shall endure them a King
first hand
a leader who too seeks
to find "The Way"

and the ransom the King asks of them
is that of the valor of their Sons
and the innocence of their Daughters
and the Virginity of their Hopes and Dreams
of a better way

and they, my children
when the burden
becomes more than what they can bear
they will turn unto me
Source
offering supplications and praise
that i might hear their calls
and their prayers

i will let them drink
once again
from the fountains of my spirit
where unblemished
pristine waters
flow

they may be refreshed
in the know
that it is not i

who have forsaken them
but they turned their face
away from that of thine own
they did not seek My Face

and i shall show My divine presence
the full splendour of My Glory
in the smiles of their children
and the warmth of their hearts
their compassion
and their tenderness
towards one another

i shall reveal unto them
that Gift which they in their blinded way
they never saw
for their eyes were darkened
with lusts of self-understanding

i shall whisper
to the hearts that long
for the answers to life's riddle
that in the middle of where thou dwells
where all is sacred
i dwell
there Am I
the King you sought

I Am thou ... and Thou Art I

They would have a King

Ultimately

my words are not shared
for the purpose of entertaining you
though you may find some musing within them

nor are my words offered for the purposes
of sustaining you
that you must do for yourself
get your God to help
whatever that may be
or whom He / She or It
is to you

my words reflect my pathway
my thoughts
my feelings
the floors
my ceilings
i experience
throughout my journey

some may say it is my struggle
that is ok
for they are right
the days
the nights
i travel
are that of my own

they may be somewhat recognizable
perhaps
but don't even try
to walk my path
find your own tours
and enjoy the sightseeing
you are paying for

whether by bus or train
the pain of its brevity
leads not to any particular levity
worthwhile
though we smile anyway

we tell stories
"Fish Stories" i think
to others and our selves too
about the Fairies and Elves we conjure
to make our lives dismally magical

i once did find a 4 leaf clover
and many 3 leaved ones i split
to sometimes 4
and many times more
as i dreamed of the possibilities
of deliverance

to where from what
ha ha ha

heaven some may call it
me, i just don't know
though
many claim they do

i think that is what Faith covers
the ambiguity of the unseen
unknown
while we lazily await a harvest
from some seeds sown
yet we keep not the garden
with the same ardent behavior
with which we dream
do we ?
pardon me . . . .

and Ultimately
whatever that signifies
there may be truth
and many misogynistic lies
we happily hug and cling to
and we are not that much different
are we

wanting what is the Ultimate
but we really do not want to face it
with any semblance of finality
though we pretend to chase it

we would rather dream
and create visions of pretense
while sitting on the fences
of the defenses
of the self-pretenses
colored by lore handed down
passed around
from ear to ear
fear to fear
tear to tear

is that queer or what
the butt kissing
and licking
and my bic is not flicking properly
cause it is made in Taiwan
yet Opie and Ron
Howard that is
are one and the same
though the names may differ
to feed you disconnectedness

and during this mess
as our ships are listing
threatening to drowns us
thus, we are poor swimmers
when it gets right down to it
bottom dwellers are we ?
perchance ?

so ultimately
let me dance
as the clown in the court
a Jester gesturing
giving life the "Bird"
and those things i once heard
let me forget them as well
and then
at least ultimately
i will be present

ultimately

The visions of a fool

Old men dream they can run again
Little boys dreaming of becoming me
Young men dreaming of skirts

Life is an unequivocal wonder
Filled with inevitabilities
That are realized far too soon

We purse elusive truths
Beckoning our paths to reconcile our desires
But "Truth" knows not of the character of "Mercy"

The toils we suffer
Perhaps lend a compassion
Perhaps not
It does yet serve the soft-hearted
He who seeks a spiritual epiphany

They say "Grace" visits the abode of the meek
Those who have lost their "Warrior Spirit"
Seeking no more the conquest
Content to abide
Side by Side
In the reflective face of their hunger
And thirsts

Isaiah called out the words
In prophesy he uttered
"Come"
Come and buy milk with no money
Eat, Drink 'til thy Soul is Fat

Who is the fool that has visions of strength
To overcome the balance
Of that which is Eternal ?
Shall the child tip the scales,
And give favor
To the weary ?

I close my eyes
And visit upon the darkness
Holding to my delusion
While hoping to conjure a silence
Where the voices rival not
Any more.

The Visions of a fool

the universe replete, thus i speak

the beast stands beside me
a dimension apart
whispering in a language
veiled
in the cloakings
of resonant memory

i hear the tone
and it strikes a chord
that calls forth the warrior
whose days of dormancy
has come to an end

what shall come of
what i have come to know ?
the question fades
with the urgency
of task
so i ask not anymore

before me stands the quest
to aright that which is askew
with me
and all the crooked paths
become straightened

there is no anger
nor penchant for balance
just retribution
for the eons of torture
the innocent child have suffered

but a bite i took
of that spoiled fruit
which compelled me
to adventure beyond the knowing

and the sowing of seed
i have done
attempting to resurrect the glory
i once held
that was stolen
and bestowed upon my brother
of the shadows
all because
of that simple misdeed
was for naught
thus far

how i long to drink again
from that place
where the four rivers
converge in the garden
that my soul may find its clarity,
but i was cursed
for my innocent offering,
banished to wander
in a realm not of mine own.
had i known . . . would i have ?

we have erected towers
in our feeble attempts
to return home
and they spilled the people like me
upon the land of dreams
and we awakened

with "Babel"~ing tongues
of understanding

we built altars
offering our obeisance
and they turned their back upon us
and they called themselves Gods?
this is when i asked the question
"to what, to whom do we serve?"

i suffer this anguish daily
meeting the Sun each morn
with a truth
that i must endure the game
yet another cycle of time
and my soulful query of "Why"
seems to fall on the ears of the deaf

i have offered penance
i have offered stripes
i have offered love
but there is naught they wish for
for they have many souls
who are all too willing
to do their vain bidding
and to be their sacrificial lambs
so my blood is not required . . .
here

they find pleasure
in the songs of the Righteous
and the lament
of their daily toils
and we erect symphonies of anguish

praying that Prime will intercede
and we plead
and we plead
and we plead

in the interim of space
that place where
light is swallowed
where the hollowness does exist
in the abyss
of nothingness
we send our hopes
to be vanquished
that it too,
and the future of our children
be not eaten
for though we are not beaten, yet
we have let
the deceits overcome us
and now we ask
in what God do we trust

in the cavity of creation
where the breath of the Holy
was implanted
we aspire to ride the ether
of our inspiration
that we may transmute
the power of Soul Speak
that others may hear
and set free their fear
to no longer roam
in their own houses
that they may visit upon

the domiciles of these false warlords
and collect their reciprocal bounties

i am removing the shackles silently
deliberately
that they not notice
as i unblind my singular eye

and i now see clearly
the disparity
which we once called our verity
our truth

now the winds of solace
dance playingly
with the unified consciousness
of the people
and we all begin to sense
a greater presence
coming
summing up our wantings,
that which is no longer appeased
in, nor with empty prayers
that were never heard

and that which we thought
and was taught
was once the beast
has long ceased its whisperings
for the voice i now hear
is that same holy breath
infused in me
and my fear is loosed

and now i have come,
i no longer dream
of empty things
i need not the Law of Attraction,
for within this fraction of existence in me
that small morsel of Prime
is mine

and i am
the universe replete
thus i speak

the words

do you still remember the words

to the Declaration of Divinity

"I AM"

do they still resonate with you

in you

through you

will you be you

when you

speak them

tell me

do you remember

the words

the Saints Walk By

the Saints are walking in the Holy Parade
playing the music we hear
whispering and singing and shouting and screams
within our dreams
wanna play ?
charades is the game of choice
in this game we call life

i pick up the blade, the knife
i attempt to consciously disengage
my consciousness . . .

the Spider Web of Doctrines and Beliefs
and the Foods of my Ancestors . . .
have i overeaten ?
they do say you are what you eat

but . . .

what was in that Casserole ?
my stomach hurts mommy
here she says . . .
take another pill
it will be all right in a little while

i trusted her
i trusted in the intentional goodness
and i am now contentionally weeping
in my soul
seeking resolve
as i evolve

the next day i fell
i skinned the knees of my divine self
i bled
they gave me a Band-Aid and some orange stinging liquid
that shit hurt !

must we be pained to heal ?
yet i am still bleeding
and the blood pours forth every day
by now i should be dead
for i have been bleeding it seems
since the beginning of time

my hands have been pierced in the palms
i can no longer grasp any truth
or any thing else for that matter

yes, i too bear a cross
upon which many times over i have been nailed

i look down from my perch of forsakenness
and i see yet still
the Saints Walk By

Utopic Dreams . . . a Memorial Day Salute

when it comes to Memorial Day
you may say
that i am not appreciative
and i am not
and i have not forgot
those who have sacrificed
their lives
that we may
hold on
to the standards of our living
our civility
humanity
our insanity

how many times can my child die
for your madness
and how many times
will we embrace this sadness
we acquiesce to
comply to
die for
and sometimes
vie for

i cry for my Utopic Dreams
that seems
to be lost

i am one
who can never condone a war
of any type
when it comes

to the taking of life

you see
they are my Brothers
my Sisters
who died
on both sides

Mothers lamenting
the loss of their sons
the lands of the people
raped
because of greed

take heed my friend
for we need to amend
our ways
our thoughts

and i know
there is always that one
that shining Asshole
somewhere
who convinces the people
of their sovereignty
that this is a thing
War
we must do
i beg to differ

yes,
The Hitlers must be stopped
popped
cropped

as well as the Noriegas
the Idi, the Amins
the Bushes
who go unseen
because we are blinded
by a term
we have come to endear
called "Patriotism"

and what about all those would be Khans
who wave that magic wand
through the news
to alter the views
persuading the people
to forget their humanity
yes … dammit
it's insanity
that we would listen
don't we know better by now ?

and your Sacred Texts
are full of such accounts
of people
who kill in the name of …

defaming my spirituality
and i can only SMDH

Holy War …
you gotta be kidding me
more like Holy Shit Batman
i can't believe they believed it …
Comical

and what about those
whose toes
never touch the field of battle

they but dictate
how you should lose your life
and why

and i ask "Why"
as my soul cries these tears
with no resolution

and get a 3 legged pony
for that crippled spirit
Joseph Kony
tie him to it
and shit
along with his dark cross
of despair
for all the souls
who are deprived
the air of life

they do this
because they have an agenda
that is not to your best interest
did you hear what i said

THEY DON'T DO IT FOR YOU !!!!!
but you have been elected
selected
to die for them
AHEM

and History continually recycles itself
changing Uniforms and Names
and Geographics
that we not clearly see
we do not have to die for them
for you
for me

we can choose to live
if we but stop the hate
and learn to love
self and others
for in the end scheme
just like Martin's dream
we are all
Sisters and Brothers

and the Lenins
who be beginning
these surges
of frivolous mouth frothing madness
of people against people
perhaps i shall pray for them
perhaps not

but right now
all i can do is "Imagine"
isn't that what Lennon said
but he is dead now
or is he ?

the Caesars
the pleasers
the Republicans

persuading the Publicans
from Christ to Rome
from Doctrine
to Dome
the Rote
the Rites
that usher forth Night
steal our Children's Suns
and if you blink your eye
another War has begun
somewhere

so memorial day is here
and i pray i remember
the value of life
the smile of a Son
and it's meaning to his Mother
his Children
the World
that shall never see it again

may these words be my memorial
and thus become a reality
where our frailties
our propensity
to kill each other
my Sister my Brother
show up no more

Memorial Day . . . Remembering Eden

Utopic Dreams

Dedicated to my Children's unknowing smiles

there are small slivers of light

there are small slivers of light
that pierce the shadowed fabric
that envelopes
our conscious memories
of bright times past

i try to hold on to them
and entomb them in my presence
like the present that they are
for they have an ability
to make one feel good

but they do not last
nor do they anchor themselves
to my "here" consciousness
for my convenience
that i may always wear a smile

they say i should live in the "NOW"
that is what people who proclaim
a certain evolvement will tell you,
but dammit . . .
the "now" is not all
it is cracked up to be
is it?

with the challenges we all must face
the despair we all must taste
closes in on us
stealing what little space
we once reserved for our joys

and truthfully
it is not all about me
but . . . then again my friend
it is

but i question
how can i be
so happily evolved
when the resolve
of my brothers and sisters
hangs in such a frail balance

the maladies of mankind
are often unkind
to our souls
our hearts
our minds
and anything else
us humankind
use to embrace
and cherish

people are hungry
stricken with war and famine
politics
and global economics
to name a few

i wonder if our Gods knew
this would be the road
we would have to endure
and i ask
where is the cure
for this illness

that blights our goodness
that at one time
we so freely shared

i let the lantern be enlightened
that my mind's eye
may see the path before me

if but for a few more paces
a few more steps
and my anguish shall find rest
for a moment or so

who knows
what is to come
evolve
as we let go
de-involve our spirits
from this empirical entanglement

the horsemen come
can you hear the hoof beats
the promise of a replete-ness
that will hopefully extricate us
from this mess
we have made in God's Cosmic kitchen

we spend far too much time bitchin'
about that which we have created
don't we

and it is we
who reconfirm its dire need to exist
by doing nothing

to evoke change
while stroking
our Egoic nature
with diversion
and masturbatory reason
as we seek a pleasing
that can never come
to any sort of orgasmic epiphany
that will sustain our bliss

so we seek dark places
within
and without
fearing our own reflections
for such is he
who wishes not to confront
their ultimate
reality

would that be you my friend
would that be me
that seeks to hide away
from those Divine Messengers
the Horde of Hermes
who brings to us all
a purse from the Sow's Ear
which holds within
the pearl of wisdom
that shines as a
small sliver of light
and our cosmic psyche is pierced

there are small slivers of light

what we are becoming

the light was fading from her eyes
and we all knew it
we called the malady Cancer

her Soul was being reassigned
she feebly protested
as life tested her resolve
and ours as well

i never could quite put it all together
and still reason wrestles in the shadows
as that proverbial enemy is never conquered
the one named "Why"

perhaps that is the quest
to awaken the souls of men
to question again
the fabric of existence

i think God likes the attention
not to mention . . .
the prayers

somewhere within me
prevails a sarcastic tone
that emanates from my own personal bell
in my own personal steeple
that rings daily
many times disturbing my peace
my sleep
my solace

the children at times seem to be lost
in a convoluted query
of which none may answer to
not even self

perhaps self-acceptance
will dull the pain of absence
who really knows

they have plenty of doctrinal pills
one can swallow
but eventually,
they all come out the other end

for me, i have this
words of empty reflections
and circumspections
which recycle themselves daily
eating the fruit of their own seeds

needs . . .

what are they ?

is it the batteries fault ?
or the manufacturer ?
perhaps that is the way
it was all designed
a brief journey here
which ushers forth a thirst
to expand beyond
the perceived limitations

that is what they are
are they not ?

or should we call it an opportunity
to discover what we are becoming
beyond the realm
of what we choose to forget

what we are becoming

what is this soft voice i hear

what is this soft voice i hear

whispering sweet nothings in my ear

could it be the Voice of Poetry

beckoning me

to speak of her beauty

to be who i am

4 + 7
i'm squaring heaven
craps shot 11
and i am still eating
unleavened bread

in respite's sweet sorrow
far off is the morrow
and its potential horrows
still loom in my head

we hold to our fears
counting them dear
ain't that shit queer
we live to play dead

change your thoughts they say
this is a brand new day
make a new path, new way
in my new shoes built of lead

yet still have i desires
fueled by the fires
as i continually aspire
my divine wings to spread

so i will not bereave
when i can conceive
that i too achieve
as i rise up from my bed

for i am a Son
kissed by the Sun
Universally One
i shall not be afraid

i shall extract this dead
out of my head
take off my shoes of lead
my wings be spread
spit out sorrow's bread
to my dreams be wed
cause i am not afraid
to be who i am

My Brother June Barefield triggered this as reflected in the Open Stanza.
His Profile Pic displayed a 5/4 and i had to go in to it . . .
i came up with a bit more of me.

Bless up my Brother June

without tears

skins and layers have encapsulated my memories
and i was peeling this onion
with a tearless disdain
refraining from an emotional investment
in this testament
to self

i wanted to see
if it was my fault
or the circumstance
happenstance
afforded my path
yeah . . . shit happens

they say that life is fair
i can buy that,
but sometimes
people need a break
for they, we
were not prepared
to travel this journey
without a map
so we are expected to get lost
at times
aren't we ?

there have been many wrong turns
i think,
but with perspective
i do have the choice
to look at them differently
don't i ?

these supposed wrong turns
have brought me to this point
of reconciliation
hasn't it ?
if i could but gather the lessons
and apply them forward

yeah, i am confessing
to some degree
that i need some help

perhaps a little Cosmic understanding
is now due
for me
for you
and the world

and now here i sit
peeling the onions
trying to get a peek
at what lies beneath the skin
what lies within
at the core of things

and i shall not shed a tear
i shall remain staunchly clear
embraced by resolve
to overcome the fears
that impeded me from doing this
so many times before

i do not wish to be blinded anymore
by my own bull shit
nor convenient delusions

we at times cosign
and label them as an illusion
created by others
don't we ?

but this day
i am confronting me
and i but want to see
who i truly am
if i can but finish
peeling this onion
called "ME"
without tears

who really understands ?

who amongst us truly understands
the path of a man
we call brother

who truly can feel
the pain another
endures

we go about our lives
insulated
for we have our own issues
and woes
dancing in our thoughts

we sometimes employ our toes
to dance
that we may perhaps
dance our spirits away
far away
where we can no longer hear it
the cries of that inner child
for solace
understanding
and comfort

where we may
escape from the ghosts of darkness
that haunts all souls of light

and some
do
believe they are not

and cannot be
frightened
but the auspiciousness of life
and i smile for them
for even in their delusions
they seem to be ok
for a while

others of us
have given up
attempting to reconcile
and reassemble the puzzle
of reasonable divinity

and with undue affinity
we yet still meander down crooked paths
we see as straight
but straight unto what i ask ?

i look to my left
and i sense pain
through my eyes
and they are open
for a moment
but i have to close them
and seek that place
that place of dreams
so i can face
all that seems
displaced in this heaven i desire

the fire i once avidly stoked
as a youth
quietly burns

with a sort of ambient glow
and most times i am content
to sit and watch the licks of flame
flicker
from orange to yellow to blue to red
and sometimes green
for there is still yet much
we have not seen
will we ever ?

and as clever as we may think we are
or i am
or wish to be
there is an looming uncertainty
as to where this path truly leads

yes like you too
i know what i have been told
and all i embrace as possibility
was put in the fold of "knowledge"
by someone else
who perhaps too
stood on this same precipice of self
seeking answers

and in the end of it all
wherever that may be
call it the land of the free for some
purgatory for others
i ask again
this simple question
for that other man
who resides in me
as well... who really understands ?

Today i Teach

Today i Teach

Tomorrow i Learn

if one knows nothing

then what is there to teach

but emptiness

when one achieves

the State of Emptiness

and non-Knowing

One can be filled with the "Is"-ness

of all things

Today i Teach

Tomorrow i Learn

the Road

the Road to Destiny is filled with Doubt and Fear
the Road to Joy goes Far and Near
the Road of Life is sometimes Queer
the Road to Nowhere starts Somewhere

the Road of Content is all Down Hill
the Road of Success Failure Fills
the Road to Understanding Silence Tills
the Road to Peace has many Kills

the Road to Happiness is how you Perceive
the Road to Truth is what you Believe
the Road to Enlightenment is how you Conceive
the Road to Love is given not Achieved

the Road back Home requires a Sight
the Road to Self is littered with Blight
the Road to Oneness travels the Night
the Road to God is found bathed with Light

the Road i travel is within Me
for on my Road "i" now am Free
i now have garnered a new decree
to be to others what "I" wish to be

on the Road . . .

would we do it ?

he wasn't a bad guy
just a guy
trying to make the best of things
in his life

yes, there were challenges
and troubling times as well
and many things
he just had to let go
for he surmised
either
he had no control over them
or the effort was too great
for what was to be gained

and no one offered to walk in his shoes,
not that he would let them.
they would probably . . .

he, over his lifetime
had adopted many personal credos
to address his adopted perspectives
to survive
himself

some offensive
EXTREMELY !!!
and others were just the
"get over yourself"
type of affirmations

a few perhaps are worth mentioning
such as
"you don't want to be on the tracks
when this train comes out of the station"
now he laughs at his arrogant insensitivities
or
"either help me get where i am going,
or get the fuck out of my way"
That really says it all
even to this day
though the words are softer,
the intent is the same

then there was
"no expectations, no disappointments"
this came from his low level of faith
in the people around him . . .
not much has changed
i think

he had an affinity for
Descartes'
"cogito ergo sum"
he found resolve in his thinking
most times,
but . .
"all things are possible"
kept his psychic boat afloat
yes
this allowed him
to get beyond the Bullshit

self-induced
and otherwise

as time continued forward
he was losing his proclivity
for affirmations
and in summation
he was simply content
to be . . that is
2 "BE"

sort of like a wait and see game
testing his faith i guess

you know . . .
sow the seeds
and see what comes of it

i wonder at times
does he really even have a clue ?
just like the rest of us
"if we only knew what we could do"
would we do it ?

they were right

there are faint voices
whispering
bidding to be heard
but fear rebukes them
for the busy souls of us
who have no time
to listen

we dress our pains so prettily
with polite smiles
and polite gestures
of acceptance
acquiescence
for ostracization
is but another
stake
in our hearts
of misunderstanding

all we vied for
and thus will ultimately
die for
is but a sweet meaningful embrace

a loving ingratiation
and appreciation
for who we are
within
inside
where we hide
and thus call our inner child

and the anguish of this child
is ever vigilant
diligent in its seeking
for absolution
a reparation of the ages
that neither priests
nor sages
really quite acknowledged
nor wished to speak on
teach on
preach on
for it negated their need
amongst the common people

they built steeples
with loud bells
so that you could find them
upon the calling
the ringing
of the bell

your bell
our bell
makes no difference
for their was Dogma
to preach about
teach about
and tell
over and over again
to us parishioners
until
we believed exactly
what they wished for

bring your offerings
to the Altar
and let us alter you
neuter you
spiritually
all checks and cash and credit cards
accepted
without exception
the grand deception

Pulpits and Pews
and Thrones
for the King of the people
and Altars too
made in China
maybe Taiwan
or Malaysia
Korea
or the good ole USA
with imported woods
should you think
it was not exotic enough
for your Custom Designed God
but don't forget your check books
and before you leave the house
check looks
in the mirror
for there is a standard
to maintain here

now on with the Sermon of the Week

there once was a guy named Herman
who the people believed a Vermin
cause he did not remit
nor submit to the shit
that we were so damned determined
to believe
cause we needed to believe
just to make it through the day
cause those damn voices
were whispering again
that we had lost our way
a long time ago

and didn't you know
they were right
they were right

will that do for you?

i bowed
in the deepest of reverence
for i had an offering

within my hands
there was my heart
and i offered it to life
that i may fully live

i knew naught of anything else
save Trust
for God was seen
in all things
within
and without

i felt the Presence of the Greater
in my thoughts
my intent
my deeds
my wishes and visions too
which is why
i have always sown seeds like this
to touch needs like this
in myself
and possibly you too

i remember,
do you . . .
when we did not carry heavy things
upon our shoulders of reason
but somehow

we reasoned that "Gift of Conviction" away
while trying to adapt
and please others

many times i asked myself
why do i bother
and i realized
i was afraid of the loneliness
of walking my own path
with no crowd cheering
no naysayers jeering
validating my rights
to rebuke them
as i refuted my own glory
of being
can you see
where i am going with this ?

i remember when life Kissed me
. . . often
daily
and i kissed her in return

her very breath was my lover
and she reminded me
of our bond of joy
with every heartbeat

take a seat here son
i have a story to tell
one for the ages
one that all the Sages speak of
about the Love

*you see
a long time ago
more than we now know
there was this place
that was not a place at all
until the call came
in the name of you
the name of me
and we
shall call Him, She, It Father
or whatever you wish or rather
for the words, they really do not matter
but they "DO"
yes words "DO"!*

*He spoke those words
"Let It Be"
famous now
and somehow
life began
Man will never quite understand
or will he
the Power of the Word that "BE"
can you see
what i am saying here*

*and from that point on
there was not only the Dark
but the Dawn
that we,
would have something to live for
vie for
as we look for
that door*

to our liberation
from our own ghosts,
our exacerbation
from the deliberations
we hold as truths in our reason
season in . . . season out

and through each day of our lives
the Sun does rise
we still bring doubts to the table
feeding the lame and the able alike
while disabling
becoming the less
than valiant dreams
within and without

it is our own very psyche
that deludes us
as we have lost our trust
in the greater of things
we once knew so intimately

so we invented Faith
that we may believe
in that which we conceive
oh the woe in that statement

we are told
and reminded that
if we believe we can achieve
such things
we use to just speak of and see
as we watched them actualize
before our eyes

before the advent of time
did arise
to interrupt our flow
of what we once took for granted
"The Know"

i ask you
did you know that . .
You are God manifest ?

That is the test of all souls
to come to realize
that the stories you are told
are just that "Stories"
Fables and Lies
whether White or Black
they are all cute diversionary synonyms
to keep you separated from Him
or Her
or It
shit
awake
for goodness sake
awake my child

well, back to the Garden
where the fruit is sweet
and you are complete
in the knowing
that you are the Wind
the Moon
the Stars . .
you are the Near, and the Far
the seen embraced

in what is not readily faced

dare i impugn
that you are all things
that's a twist on logic
for you "Are"
but simply listen to this
you are
God Manifest
and Ordained
it's plain you see
if you choose to
simply Be

let me take task here
and simply ask you dear
If that which is "Perfect" created a thing …
what is that thing ? …
can it be any less ?

Let us stop all this confessing
to unknown Sins
we are born in
again and again
and gather the lesson
and get off this deluded Merry Go Round
where all are Dizzy
and busy
creating Haunted Houses and rides
for you to be induced to abide
and be absently happy
with the doled out Candies
Cottony and soft
dreams aloft

with our commitments to truth
aloft as well
while we scoff and tell
more nursery rhymes
to the children

the Son does go down
at this Circus
where all the Clowns
with Scary, Silly faces of surreal Truths
continue the venue
of make believe
and we are entertained
and we remember our pain
don't we

yes . . . let us "Make Believe"
that we are free
to be what we wish to be
Happy dammit

will that do for you ?

what i am

i am still being discovered
uncovered
bared
exposed
as the skirts of possibilities
are being lifted
and my position
is shifted
that i may have
a peek

i speak
with many tongues
all are true and direct
none are forked
that you may detect
who i am

i am a collection
of vibrations
whose congruous essence
has been gathered
and slowed down
that you may see me
and enjoy my presence
as i do yours

First Father
Progenitor
Source
spoke
and evoked a magic

He said
"Let there be"
and i was
as dust in the wind

i settled

the word of creation
formed a resonant vibration
and it fell down
to the ground
to form this mound
you call earth

I am the Great Mother
and She is me
and you

the Hands of Father
picked me up
and spat upon me
and molded me
to become a shaped
entity
with a definitive
density
an enmity
you can hold on to
so hold me

i have Cosmic Consciousness
enfolded in me
in my DNA you see
that emboldens me
to know
that life is as i deem it to be
so i flow with it
go with it
shit
i am it
you are it
for i
you
we
speak it
every day
every way
when i say
anything

so say something good
would you

could you
can you
imagine
the wonder
of perfection

it is our election
our choice
our free will
our voice
the fountains of actualization

that alters the vibration

it moves the mountains
or makes them
out of mole hills
laced with our ills
as we turned our powers on
and direct them
errantly
fearingly
towards one another
instead of with
one another
our Brothers
and our Sisters
it is but the wrong preposition

and if we were even
to consider
the pre-position
of our supposition,
the if in
"to be" in
the you and i
in we in
we could alter
the condition
of our self-made
perdition
we so often bitch about
no doubt
what do you think

do we even think enough
or too much

these are but extremes
of our actualized dreams
which seems
to be out of control . . .
but is it ?

we act as if
we are here
just for a visit

so we take no responsibility
for the frailty
and the lack of
our civility
within us
within humanity
as we seek to quantify
our own vanity
claiming a sense of sanity

WOW

so now the inane
rules the day
it's insane
isn't it
what do you say
shit ?
what next

wait a minute . . .
i'll get back up in it
but let me
answer this text message first

it's from God
He's telling me
what i am . . .

listen . . . .

this is a dumb ass poem for all the dumb ass people

for all the dumb asses who think having millions of dollars is not enough
for all the dumb asses in uniform who misuse their power and position
for all the dumb asses who covertly or openly seek to exploit their fellow human being's weaknesses
for all the dumb asses with the letters behind their names that believe that makes them smarter or of better ilk than those without
for all the dumb asses who have it to give and close their hands and their hearts
for all the dumb asses who would take the life of another human being arbitrarily
for all the dumb asses who create wars to further covert agendas
for all the dumb asses in politics who don't give a flyin' fuck about the people they serve
for all the dumb asses who abuse children, women and each other
for all the dumb asses who marginalize themselves and their fellow humans deliberately
for all the dumb asses who sit in judgment and are blinded for their heads are stuck up their own dumb asses
for all the dumb asses that think the colors of their skins, their politics, their religion, their economics provides them some sort of advantage that should be exploited over others
for all the dumb asses who think they are better than someone else
for all the dumb asses who do not recognize they are dumb asses like me
for all the dumb asses who do know they are dumb asses and take pride in being the dumb asses they are . . . like it's cute or something

we thank all you dumb asses because it is your dumb asses that are causing us dumb asses to wake up and get rid of your dumb asses

this is a dumb ass message from one dumb ass to another

this crushed heart

my heart has been crushed
by the weight of its burden
and the tethers of expectations
have come undone

the free fall was exhilarating
but somewhere in the recesses
of all reason
i knew that gravity
would eventually
have dominion
over this fanciful
state of consciousness

call it an awakening
if you will...
for me i was
i am
for the impact of reality
the grounding of me
quite astoundingly
made me aware
that the sleep
would not endure
could not secure
me

i am a million pieces of thought
scattered across the landscape
of "Why Me~s"
yes, why me
why did i have to be disturbed
to what sanction about me
must i adhere
that i have forgotten

is there a lesson
of any profundity
to be acquired ?

perhaps it is hidden
beneath her skirt
just like all the other delusions
i have peeked at
over this journey

funny
the masturbatory games we play
daily
clinging to ghosts
of our own spiritual makings

no faking a truth you know
they have no substance
one can cling to
save that of what is conjured

will a smile make the pain ease ?
will it usher forth
that which appeases the soul of men ?

we know not
or do we
we pretend
that we always knew we
had a power we
were not ready to handle

and now i fumble through the twilight
feeling
searching
for that candle
that i may bum a light
from someone
won't you assist me
or just kiss me
if you would
and perhaps . . .
perhaps
i can re-inflate
this crushed heart

the widow

a widows web is weaved
with lamentations and memories
and sprinkled trinkets
that glisten
and transform into
fleeting warm smiles

we try to hold on
but the delicacy of times past
that which did not appear
at those moments
as authentic
has now transmuted to treasures
we fight to conjure into our lives
on a daily basis

dare i not forget

the children serve as reminders
with their anguish cloaked
with reason
and distraction
of the day

yes we are lost
in a new wilderness
seeking a way
to resolutions we abhor

we send seemingly meaningless wishes
into the ether
hoping that lore was true
that there is a heaven
and again
i shall be with you

but now i am but a widow
weaving a web
to hold to these memories
in my heart
in my head
when i was alive
and not just

the Widow

the Storm is coming

i stand in reverence
watching the changing of the guard
as the heavens above me
begin to speak of what is to come

the clouds become ambiguous
submissively relinquishing
their personal definition
to a great presence
that not so silently approaches

they enjoin to speak
with one ominous voice
as the Storm begins
to make her presence known

Brother Wind wisps in
tickling the leaves of the Trees
awakening them from their slumber
as they prepare to withstand
or yield
as will be told
with "Storm's" fury
or her gentle caress

they applaud

i smell the scent of Nature
in the air
as the once fair day
gives way
to the need of expression
found in the loud voice
of the thunder

there are flashing lights
in the distant skies and
i am in awe
as the horizon
beams with a wonder
we often do not see

the soft pitter patter of rain
walks in softly
touching all that it can
the leaves
the ground
and me
who is grounded as well

be still

that is what Grandma used to say
she even prayed
at these times in my younger life

somehow
i forgot the drill
but today
i too shall spill my heart
my thoughts
and let them go back
from whence they came

and perhaps a name to call
will come to me
as they have done
for Grandma
that name that gave her a peace
that was stilled

when Storms did come

what it is

there are old tongues
that speak of
old days
to fresh minds
of old ways

we are enchanted
eyes mesmerized
by the lore
as we recognize
truth
which cannot be
recanted
from reality

children of Source
seeking a light
that can only be embraced
tasted
faced
by pure hearts

Souls are aching
for reconciliation
to their higher selves
a place of knowing
where a wonder
for what has transpired
throughout the aeons
brings forth a certain reverence

for life
the rife
of creation

the magnificent songs
of expressive beauty
are constantly sung
in our movements
our thoughts
our intent
our dreams

we are
what we were meant to be
a human
humane development
manifesting itself
unto a higher state of glory
as we grown a new sort of wings

we tell the stories
to our children
performing incantations
of expectations
and we shall fulfill them
just ask God
he gave the nod
that this may be
when He said
"let there be"
see

so i am where and what i am
as are you
true and sure
no flaws
cause
we be pure
and we will endure
the illusions
for they will fade
as do all temporal things
can you hear the singing ?

and the ancients come
and revisit us
bless us
through the veils
through our words
our feelings
our intuitions
bringing forth fruition
of the 1st dream
as He did deem
it to be so

so let's get with it
and speak of the old ways
in the new days
and get back to what it is

i stand not alone

call me delusional
but i stand not alone

there is a place
that haunts some resonant memory
embedded in me
perhaps it is a DNA thing
who knows

it tells me that
there is something within me
that is greater than my delusions
and it faintly whispers to my soul
beckoning me to awaken
and return . . .
home

i stand not alone . . .

i look upon the fabric of our existence
and the consistence
of absence
is stark
in this dark resemblance
of our semblance
of "life"
but life abundant
only peeks through
every once in a while
did you see the greater too ?

i stand not alone . . .

last night i sat and i asked myself

if we are co~creators
that is what i surmise
for so many things
i have thought
and spoke
did come to fruition

and it is now time
to examine
my seditious ways

so...
last night i sat and i asked myself

these words that i speak
these words that i pen
do they offer any amends
to the ills i speak of

do they heighten my sense
our sense
of love
and the power it can be
for you
for me

or am i just making commentary
on the things
we already know

last night i sat and i asked myself

am i serving a valid purpose
beyond my own
co-created validities
the conformity
of my delusional normality
or is this but another face
of my frailty
and the things
i can not quite grasp
as reality

the milk has spilled
and i cry over it
when i should be getting
over it
and seeking
some sort of resolution

solutions are what we need
will poetry
bring this about
help us mitigate the doubt
that things will ever
get better
because of the words
we spout
or shout

is hope enough
is message enough
is verse enough
to disperse
the terse
attitudes we see about us
between us

last night i sat and i asked myself

if "once upon a time"
things were different
then what, who and when
spawned the indifference
amongst us

last night i sat and i asked myself

what am i going to do ?
write another Poem ?

last night i sat and i asked myself
and then . . . i wrote this

metaphorically speaking

metaphorically speaking
my felicific meanderings
and masturbatory philandering
is best done
with my own pandering
of self

i mean . . .
if i can't get my self ON
and Off
then who can

i am ready
to pop my Betty
in Boo
and you too

you see
something within me
has been brewing
stewing
all my damn life
and i think
it is time to set the table
that we may dine

the fables of this day
we have been fed
are true
lies

the handwriting on the walls
in those holy halls
we call scripture
verse
that was dispersed
for man to ingest
was but a test
to see if we were listening

let he who has an ear hear
is what he said
yet we kept
regurgitating
the agitating doctrines
and teachings
for they disturbed
our sense of peace

but you knew
like i knew
that the day would come
when all this bullshit
had to cease
yes we knew
like Agnew knew
that's what Gil Scott said

that song plays over and over
in my head
sometimes

yes sometimes
we do have those epiphanies
disturbing our delusional symphonies
and we get on our knees to pray
pleading for our anguish to stop

pour some milk on it
as we listen to the
Snap, Crackle and Pop
and just like Rice Crispies
they ain't crispy no more

like whores on the first of the month
we think we got it goin' on
getting paid
to get laid
but again
like Gil spoke
"did you hear what they said"

choke on that shit

another song of reckoning
playing between my ears
skipping recordings
beckoning me
and you too dude
to stop feuding
and fighting
with our higher self

we have been looking for treasure
and misguided temporal pleasures
when the Gold of Soul
was always within
is that the original Sin ?
Lorde help us

and we are still raiding
that damn Tree
in the Garden
blaming it on Satan
that's what Flip quipped . . .
"the Devil made me do it"

like the only Cock in the Chicken yard
we the Bards of expressions
are parading vibrantly
teasingly
as we mock God himself
with our terse verse

please, get a grip
or you will be back again
for the next trip
around this damn
merry go round

like clowns in a Carnival
we have learned
to paint our own faces
crazy ain't it
makeup !

Are we the Gods
of this Breath we have
while we have it ?
is this the test
we have come to take

who will pass this "GO"
you can keep the damn $200.00
i just want out of the game
where my name is the Monopoly
of how i am identified
quantified
and thus
qualified

that guy born "me"
has died a long time ago you see
and i have been struggling fervently
to recapture that essence
the presence
of who "i" in my deepest recesses
know that i am

you see,
the "i" in me is my Cosmic Gem
and i have been mining for it
minding for it
looking aimlessly
for what i already have

and when i did open my eyes
i realized
that you had it too

we all have
that connection
without deflection
that escapes the obvious detection
that tells us of the direction
we should go

march on

and i know
you know
what i am speaking on

i think soon come the time
when rhyme will no longer suffice
nice !

better realize
before the time is gone

i'm just

metaphorically speaking

let us party

let us gather the Demons and Saints
and have a Party
after all
here is another year
where we have coexisted

the battle field is quiet now my child
as we sit and lick our wounds,
those of our reality
(if you can call it that)
and those we dream

the portents of the pretense is present
let us not hesitate
to expectorate
all that is of the "Shadow's" world
for a new Sun is being Heralded in
and the Scabs of thy Soul
will be peeled away
without empathy for your discomfort

got any aspirin ?
they told me to always take a few
before the intake
of volumous libations
and this is the situation
that calls for this precaution
for i am heading toward
that Bus Stop of Exhaustion

just another stop along the way
where the weary souls lie
waiting for
that free ride back home

but right now
no time for such heavy thoughts
i am slipping out of the yoke
and i will dance this night
with both
the Saints
and the Demons
for they both stood by me
when i needed a friend

let us party

my love for you

my love for you is unending

and when i say that

know that even God

can not contain its essence

for its essence

is God

when i think of you

i hear the regal choir

His personal cadre of voices

begin to sing

and all of existence smiles

for me

for you are the light

of my world

i want my poetry to . . .

a Rebel Poetry the chant

i want my poetry to touch your soul
i want my poetry to fill that hole in your heart
i want my poetry to move you to action
just like mr. Jackson
i want my poetry to make you stand up
be counted

yes . . .

i want my poetry
to make you rip the flesh of your delusions
from your false realities, bias and prejudice
that you may perhaps get a glimpse
of your higher self

i want my poetry
to be that key
that unlocks the chains
of your enslaved thoughts
i do hope you can read . . .
hear and listen

i want my poetry
to make your soul scream so loud
that it expands and explodes
and the noise of its voice
pollutes the world with Truth

i want my poetry
to hold the hands of your dreams
upon its breast
and for you to feel
the heartbeat of joys not yet spoken
that is labeled with your name

i want my poetry
to kiss your aspirations
with smiles of happy butterflies
that i may watch you simply dance
because you can

i want my poetry
to open the floodgates of your reason
that your limited perspectives
of difference and deference drown
in the cascade of the waters of unity

i want my poetry
to till the soils of your spiritual garden
with possibilities
and plant ever abundant new seeds
of exponential-ness
so that all previous preconceived boundaries
and limitedness
will dissipate
into the eternal ether of nothingness
and you learn to laugh at yourself
again

i want my poetry
to compel you
assist you
in the removal of your mask
to compel you to rip your clothes off
to compel you to
dance in the streets naked like David
that we, you can see who you truly are
and be affirmed that you are
fine
and
divine

i want my poetry
to teach you and me
the divine art form
and purpose
of spiritual masturbation
that we may learn
to no longer condemn the holy
which resides within each of us
and we learn to forgive ourselves

i want my poetry
to eradicate our reluctance
to love each other,
to lose the inhibitions we have been taught
indoctrinated to embrace as the right way
and learn a new way
this day
of how to love

i want my poetry
to be loving
kind
to be enduring
accepting
non-judgmental
uplifting
enlightening
embracing
empowering

i want my poetry
to reflect the beauty of creation
i want my poetry
to reflect the best of who i may be
i want my poetry
to be poetry
and help you become
a Poem

a Monte Poem Prompt

inspired by Monte Smith,
Street Poet, Activist, Humanitarian, Author, Friend

love did me in again

where is the anesthesia
i need something to dull this pain
for love has come through my door
again

she professed to have gifts of sweetness
and in my naivety
and meekness
i believed
she deceived
and now
i am in bereavement
and there is not a scent
of her presence

love,
that bitch
refuses to stitch
my self esteem back together
telling me some dumb shit
like . .
whatever
waving the hand
in my face

i need some help up in here
to understand
i have a medical plan
will it aid my illness
re-establish me

from my will –less – ness
my proclivity for the stupidity
that love brings
to our psyches
MEDICS . . .

i need medical attention
not to mention . . .

Love
she is not a doctor
nor a surgeon
and in my purging
i bleed
yes i bleed

she has ripped open my heart
and i, like a fool welcomed her
and damn . .
love
she ruled me
she schooled me
and cool me
has lost my swerve
the nerve of that . . .

i am listening

where i come from
where i been
only footprints
and memories can tell
and memories fail me
at times

where i am going
God only knows
at least that
is what they tell me

like a leaf in a Spring wind
i am disconnected from life
like a leaf in an Autumn breeze
the Trees that were once my solace
have let me go
to die
that i may serve

i look over my shoulder
at the plundered furrows
of the garden
that once bore luscious greens
and imaginations
and dreams
of past harvests
and fruits

yes, time
suits not the seeker
but it has served me well

i have gathered
collected
inspected
reflected
on more stories
that i can tell

and there are more
in that well
if not
me and my failing memory
will concoct a stew for you
to leave you wide-eyed
with awe
about all the things we saw
along the way
yesterday
and tomorrow too

how about you
do you have a story
about where you come from ?
please tell me . . .
i am listening

is it lunch time yet ?

Bologna & Bread, Mayonnaise and Butter Pickles
with Jelly, no Peanut butter on a slice or 2
for dessert

No Jelly
Alaga Syrup will do

Sandwich

and this Sand Which
is stuck in my ass
from spending
too much time at your beach
instead of my own
has always been known
to cause me issues

all in the
crack
of my toes
heaven knows
i am annoyed

who invented this shit
sand which
wasn't he an Earl or something
in an go figure
"United Kingdom"
where all of us beasts
have diverging agendas

is it lunch time yet ? . . . i'm outta here . . .

i hear you

like a reed in the marsh
wavering to and fro
in the soft Ocean breeze
i too have dreams of flying

to but embrace my Brother the Wind
and let him carry me to foreign lands
but i am rooted where i am
but i still imagine
of those things unseen

we vacillate betwixt such ends
creating our own convolutions
seeking solutions
to the seemingly impossible

my thoughts drift asunder
and my toes are stuck in the mud

the twilight approaches
the Sun of the evening
sets beyond the horizon
and gives way to the night
and the light of the Moon
draws forth the warm embrace
of the Evening Tide
as they come again
to kiss the shores of our consciousness

they come to my house
and lay gifts at my feet
tales of the travel they enjoyed

the Seas of the World
the Streams
and the Clouds of the Sky
and the Mountains and the Valleys
and we must mention the Rains
oh the Rains

i stand ever so planted
lost in the whisperings of life
and the wonder of their journey
while the tentacles of my own doing
these non-forgiving roots
which tether me to where i am
yet nurture who i am
holds me fast
where i am

the Sun of the Day
now slumbers as well
here
yet is now dancing with children
of another land
urging Workmen and Mothers
to indulge in the calling of Life
and duty
while some here sleep
but not i,
i am dreaming

i feel the nudging of my Brother, Wind
softly caressing
stirring me
reminding me
that this is not so bad
for he does bring the stories
and whispers them in my ear
and i softly reply
"i hear you"
Thank You

Metaphoric dreams

it seems like i have been dreaming about her for aeons
i often thought of what she would look like
the visions i conjured were all alluring
and moved me in ways i speak not of
save in my own private chambers
of sweaty passionate nights

speaking of nights
many of them i was rendered sleepless
hoping the phone would ring
or there would be that unexpected
yet desired
knock at my door
but it never came
but it was nice to dream anyway

it was those dreams
those damn "Someday" dreams
from Monday through Sunday dreams
that made all this loneliness bearable

yes . . . she would fix it all for me

i used to draw pictures
doodling i think they called it
shit

i could see her face clearly in my head
but i was never quite able to get it on paper
pretty much like that poem
i can not quite grasp
the non-conclusive elusive stuff

i have examined every detail of her face
her body
to include all the secret places
i would discover
that evoked her smiles and giggles
i loved when she wiggled like that
while laying next to me

i could smell her
yes smell her
and taste the texture
of her lips upon my own
who would have known
that this day would truly show up

and i think my eyes are open
for surely my nose was
i am but a mindless puppet
for her
but i don't mind
just as long as i can
hold on to my
Metaphoric dreams

of course i said it

the Cosmic Child
stood upon life's flowered pathway
vexed
perplexed
feeling hexed

he simply wanted to be happy
but he was afraid
to skip again
for he might trip
and fall again
and bust his
lip again
and bleed again
his life's blood
upon the journal
of his memories
his own diary of death
which he had to write
had to live

he has died
so many times before

each new door
he has passed through
ushered forth new beginnings
a new path

where his past sinnings
had to be let go
that he may release
all that he once
thought he knew

so . . .

life had given him a present
new toys
to build with
to deploy
a new vision
a new way
a new now
a new day
somehow

like playing with LEGOS
he constructed
new shapes
new dreams
new desires
new wants
as he let go
the tired dogma
he once believed would save him

the house of thought he inherited
from his forefathers
his mothers
were bothersome
and for some reason
every season

his storehouse felt empty
haunting
daunting
and he wanted more

he wanted more
than everything
he wanted all things
he wanted to be all
he could ever be
you see,
he wanted nothing
nothing more than to be free
detached completely
from the attachments
of things
the things his soul
never really did care about

yes, he dared not to skip
so he reverently walked
with his ever vigilant eye
watching
surmising
the surprising truths
life presented him

what was truth ?
what is this truth
that belies
beneath the surface of the Sun
the Son

what is this truth that slumbers
in a bed of lies
cloaking itself
choking our reason
till we turn blue
choking the very essence
of our joy
our lives
from our grasp

the task was his own wonder
which he embraced
longed to taste
to face
that wonder of his sweet promise
of a fruit
that his anticipatory soul
spoke of
a love abundant
without the redundant disappointments

he would not be deterred
nor deferred
and he would not skip

no he would without method
methodically
examine his potential
that exponential quality of self
he knew existed
twisted you say

well, by vision
or dream
illusions be gleaned
for it seemed to him
he must be redeemed
that he may
someday appreciate
fully
this life's flowered pathways
in full and eternal bloom
of a conscious awareness
where he can face himself
fearless
never the less
as a child of Source
without recourse
and of course
i said it !

just a write, a right

my pen wants to come out to play
what do you say
can i frolic in your garden
where consciousness visits
sometimes

my rhymes are amiss
and i tell you this
i don't give a flying whatever
about that endeavor

i am more about
how clever
my delivery may be
and what subverted messages
i can allow you to see
you see
i don't
so won't you take this
meandering journey with me
and perhaps
we can discover
uncover
something wonderful

there are profane
words
from inane mind
reminding me
of the insanity
i embrace

not often
am i so willing
to face my self
or have to taste my self
and my shit

most times
as the prosecutor, judge and jury
i acquit my self
no worry
i will be redeemed

and to those esteemed ones
like he who peers at me
in that mirror
leering at me
jeering and jibing
while i am scribing . .
go take another nap
i will call you when i am done
poking fun at us
trust me
or not

but yesterday i forgot
something
and a happy face "LOL" and hearts to you
boo
love you too

funny what one may get
when they allow
let
their pens come out to play

today ?
did we have anything significant to say
perhaps another nay
or an aye
but know this
i wrote anyway
what did you do ?

just a write a right

Mount Kyllini

the temporal fabric
cloaked the wonder of man
and consciousness
could not pierce the veil

the Seven Sisters were gleeful
for their plan
appeared to be succeeding

raining false hopes
capturing the wills of men
as nymphs do
they defiantly deceived
our aspirations
yet we reached to embrace them
and their allure
as they danced
in the cradle of the Bull

their bitterness and anguish
knew no end
since the death of Hyas
whose nobility
was their guide of a higher order

they have weeped for aeons
inside
as they exacted their misdirection
upon Father's pride
men

suicide was a consideration
when Atlas went on journey beyond
but eternity would not release them
from its grasp

so they blinded all they could see
that their errant judgments
would only be disclosed
in the inner light
of those who knew
of the legend of Arcadia
upon the Mount Kyllini

i still see Demons

you see Angels
i see Demons
schemin'
trying to figure out
how to infect
my natural psyche
with proclivities
and dogma
that your way
your religion
is better than mine

there is naught divine
about embracing
lower vibrations
of expression
and confessions
to another dense soul
will not fill that hole
that all men seek to understand
but run from

yeah, everyone
vies for salvation
from themselves
everyone
wants 40 virgins
at least the men do
i think

but what do i know
i am not your Buddha
nor an awakened one
i feel like a forsaken one
to have to endure
this cataclysmic Sun
built upon foundations
of lore
fables,
myth
stories and misconceptions
lies and deception

for real for real
i believe everyone should go with
what they feel
once they learn
to feel again
be real again
and stop stealing
other pragmatic pathways
from blind men
who have another agenda
named "Control"

what happens to the Soul
of those
who willingly gave
their juice
to be marketed and used
by those who would

make black abysmal holes
to lock you away
for another eternity

certainly
even if you had a pass
a "Get out of Jail Free Card"
you still would have to find
that cell door
and that is what Hell is for
to torment you
in your licentious ways
and lament-filled days

but now i am tired
i need answers
not romancers
of that heavy stone
that rock
that burden
i carry on the back of my dreams
for liberation

the exacerbation
is poisoning
my expectations
that any good will soon come
but i have hope

but…
in the mean time
i still see Demons

again

let us lift the veil

that the rains of reason

may pour down

and wet our consciousness

that it may bond with the liquid essence

of understanding

and learn to flow again

that we may come to

know again

the road we travel

and must go again

that we can resurrect man again

to the stature he once enjoyed

again

my brother i come to you

my brother i come to you

for i am thirsty

yet i have no money

may i sup from thy well

my sister i am hungry

will thou feed me

lay my head upon thy breast

and provide solace

to this restless spirit ?

Monsters in my closet

there are monsters in the closet Ma
yes, my closet
do you have some too

i hear them breathing
especially at night
the perfect fright time
is night time
even if the Sun is out
or is that the Son

there are monsters in my closet

i have seen quite a few of them
in my day
what say you
have you had the opportunity
to meet them
greet them
have a seat
and speak with them

they say we are the ones
who complete them
and they thanked me for
not deleting them
replete, don't you think
i do

yet in spite of their gratitude
their life-long attitude
is the servitude
of me,
yes me
you see
they make for my certainty
for would i be
who i am
without
Monsters in my closet?
would you?

they are daunting
in their haunting
as they reflect upon us
so we can detect within us
our fears
our doubts
our bouts with our humanity
and our divine sanity
that is locked
in our self-made asylums
whose walls are
waiting to be tore down

and the clowns that we are
we parge the holes
and cracks
to keep them whole

like we are under attack
and we are
by that
of our own villains
and enemies
can't we see ?
what we do to our "me"

profundity is profound

i serve the silence

within the folds of silence
there is a noise
a voice
constantly beckoning
for my reckoning
and the awakening
of my greater self

all riddles have answers
i am told
all solutions
serve the equation
for that is their duty

i am listening
and i await the lighting
of the candle
that i may remove the bushel
that all in the room may see
and again the formulas fails

where, what is that cloak
that veils the essence
of this light within
casting dispersion upon self

to what end does that serve
does it validate sin's presence
of that of the illusion

the age of confusion
is upon us
twirling and knitting
and gnarling and sitting
working convexments
around and through
the minds of men
that we may create our own delusions
by the dozens
wholesaling our souls
to the highest bidders

bloodied esteems
litter the landscapes
of the promises we dream of

for some, it is all we have left
dreams so we may think on it

so why not think on
about the uselessness
of aspiring thoughts
which are tethered
neither to deed nor intent

the jackal captures the imaginings
in the throes of carnality
revealing the futility
of our mountains of civility
laced with the bitters

the poisonous flavors
of protocol
and the call
is unanswered

so this is why
i chose the silence
though it is but another tease
i yet still seek it
here upon my proverbial knees
listening for that voice i serve
for
i serve the silence

I am listening to 'now'

I hear the muscles in my bowels
Doing its digestive duties

I hear the breathing of life,
I listen as the air rushes into my nostrils
And fill my lung cavity

I hear the beating of my heart
And its attempt to keep pace
With its own perceptions of life
And it does well

I hear the bird in the wood
Calling to the day
Letting all know that life speaks
Volumes

I hear the stillness of that very wood
And the reaching of every limb
Of every Tree
To the heavens

I hear the sneaking yet not silent footsteps of thought
Tickling my consciousness to come to play with them
This day
I smile

I hear my expectations
Wailing for fulfillment
Crying against its own limitedness to dream
So i let them go
That i may re-create them
More grander than before
And again i smile

I hear delusions being manufactured
In a concept of peace within
But is it ?

I hear your call for the same

I hear God speaking
Am i He
Am i She
Or
Am i simply me
Manifest ?

I hear the evolution of past to now
And somehow it is believable
For at one time
That now was conceivable
As it is "Now"
And hear i am
Hearing the footsteps already expressed
That i address through this time's illusion
Amidst the confusion
That which i ignored

I hear this smile on my face
Humming along
Singing the song
Of Universes yet to be born
And birth them "I" will
That we may ever seek

I hear this week is gone
Yet it is still awakening
In lessons
Yet to be embraced

I hear the approach of Chance
And i listen as it
Knocks upon the door of opportunity
And i pay attention
As they greet each other
With indifferent salutations
To the dawn

I hear the soft footsteps in the Garden
As we creep through life
Wanting to Dance
But our limbs are frozen in fear
Wanting to sing
But doubt paralyzes our voices
Yet i hear you
I hear me

I hear the calling
For sleep
And that call we all will answer
Won't we

I hear the warmth in my ears
As the blood rushes to my lobes of consciousness
To attune my listening prowess

And as i said
I hear God in all things
Do you
Are you listening
I Am
You Are
The I Am
Are we not
When we listen
Within
I am listening to now

losing the battle . . .

he held his dreams closer than reason
to him the world as he knew it
was losing the battle of importance

cleverness was overrated
no one gets out alive
we were just moved to another cell
and then the rumors started

life is like that, isn't it
you know . . . what you believe

and we approach with reverence
laced with a fear
the edge of the abyss

the voices whisper from the void
"Jump", but you aren't are you ?
You will return to the village
with another adventure story
to tell the children.

They used to call them Fables,
i call them Lies
for within me belies
a certain desperation
only the cries of a desperate soul
can abate with its rationale
and tears and cheers and laughter and smiles

a spiritual cocktail is being concocted
by some would be Teacher somewhere,
at this very moment,

one who wishes to instruct me
how to walk my path
i say, write a Book
and maybe someday
when i have time away from my life
i will read your story
that is what you want me to do isn't it
read yours and forget about my own ?

Another "Self Proclaimed Knower"
of things they have never seen
through the portal of any of their eyes.
Surprise, that is what "Id" does

when the "IS" ness of self fades
we envision.
Like Television we turn on
and what peace you had
is gone
faded
in the wisping ether
of the yesteryears of thought
no longer remembered
for the tethers of significance
are undone

we are filled with commercials
of
Prophets and Prophecies
and Legacies of times past
but what about NOW ?
i don't want to dream no more
of what may be.
Dammit . . . i am a Beetle in the Bog
please . . . "Let It Be, Let It Be"
Words of Wisdom . . .
only the "i" in Me can speak

and the irony of it all
the calling prevails
to hold on to the unseen
and he obeyed

he held his dreams closer than reason
for
to him the world as he knew it
was losing the battle of importance

not any more

i gnash my teeth upon the bone
of myself
i have already rendered my flesh apart
i am dying
leaving all evidence
of my old self behind

i can no longer fight this battle
in the bowels of my reason
where i attempt
with all due feebleness
to digest the ways of this world,
at least not that which i see
or i think represents me
and you

this is not a new trial
but the same one from of old
the one i have been scolded about
the one that makes me doubt
my own soul
and its validity
and the insipidness
i can no longer address
with my energy

my psyche is overrun
with figuring just how
right now
to make it all fit
and that shit never balances
any of my equations
until i apply
surrealities
from other dimensions
and give them life here

and fear has become my friend
for i have, like you
come to depend on its presence
and i dance
in those same halls of reason
that rebukes me
refutes me
as i temporarily
act the part
apart from me
and all i suspiciously
may desire to be

i spoke to God this morning
i think
and perhaps
He is that instinct
that speaks through the shadows
of our hauntings

eerie it is
yet today i followed,
and that shadow
became my light

the cloak of deception
i adorned
to not be scorned
by the masses of asses
i embraced,
and then i faced me
and i saw naught
but myself
in "Self's" mirror

and the flesh of past personas
melted in the face of this truth
and bone and marrow remained
as the skeletal frame work
of hardened, molded dust
and then time peeked through my eye
and i . . .
was no more
yet more than all

and now the calling of
the chaos has subsided
for where i once resided
lies ruins of who i use to think i be
"me"
and i no longer have need
to suck the marrow
from my narrow perspectives
i offer to the abyss

where naught may desist
nor resist
the coming of this age
where teachers and students
sages and disciples
you and i
can drink the spirit of the Water Bearers
as they pour their offerings
upon the earth

and for what that is worth
i hunger nor thirst
not any more

if i held your truth... my resolution

if i was the keeper of your truth
would you come to me for resolution
for in truth you know
that i am the one
the absolute one
the only one
who colors your dreams
as you do mine
no denying this
that we are the bliss
found upon the lips
that is spoken
through our kiss
divine

whisper to me please
softly upon the expectations
found within the wanting of my ears
for they wish to hear
about what is to come

tell me of thy visions
where you and i
are locked
in the embrace of eternity
me in you
you in me
thoroughly entwined
fused

that there can be no distinguishing
nor separation
of our aspirations
for love
for that is all that we are

i lay you upon our bed
in the garden of our desires
where all the fruit is edible
and divinely sweet
replete
as am i
as are you
so let us begin
to commune
and consume
the very soul of us
as the moon moves us
to become a Tidal Wave
of lust
that overcomes
all of our inhibitions
as the undulations
of your hips
and your lips
touch me in ways
for as i am the keeper of your truth
you are the keeper of mine
and my resolution
that of my soul

I am he

there it stood
like a tower of light
piercing the sky
of the horizon
enjoining imaginary heavens
to this place upon which our feet
are planted

fable and folklore
spoke of this place
a garden few have seen
from which the seed of man
had been spawned

and within
was that mythological tree
which unveiled the eye
of First Father
that He should know
of what nakedness is

David danced in the street
for he felt the unabashed joy
when kissed
by the sound of Timbrels
the music of his heart
that which is divine

Job bore
the burden of reproof
for he knew
of the sweeter fruits

that which has never been seen
nor tasted

Solomon's etheric ecstasy
his glistening wisdom
knew not of limit
and he wed himself
and consummated such union
in the inner chambers of self
his beloved

my brother Isaiah
spoke of the gates
the gates of praise
that shone
calling forth the children
to embark on the path
the journey back to the garden
back home
where there is light consciousness

he said
arise, arise
and my hallelujah
stood and spread its wings
embracing never dreamed of possibilities

my inner eye beholds that Tree yonder
how i long to put my arms
around its girth
and let the gentle breeze
of brother wind
whisper to me through its leaves

let me hear again
the sweet promise
that of the fruit we shall eat
at journey's end

St. Issa was nailed to that Tree

i but wish to climb its limbs
and lay my burdens
upon its bough
and be its rock-a-bye baby

i hear the call of the rushing waters
that of Mother's Life Blood
where the Four sacred rivers converge

let us immerse ourselves
in the cleansing waters

so . . .
i packed my bags
with emptiness
devoid of all worldly things
for the world has lost its import
and there was a bequestering for the quest
Soul was beckoning me
to that reckoning of me
unto the path . . . back
back to where myth
becomes reality . . .
back to that Garden

my heart began to ardently beat
with forgotten rhythmic excitement
filled with an anticipatory syncopation
and joys replete

the resonant harmonies of ecstasy
loomed in the air about me
and thus became my every breath
and i became life's melody

the palpitations of my heart
consumed me
completely
penetrating the womb of my very existence
like a young Virgin who looks upon
the face of her eternal lover
for the first time

take me my soul screams
unto itself
open the door
open the gate
to that arduous pathway
unto my absolution
that my final traipse
may begin

i turn my face away
from my destination
and begin to walk backwards
that i may revisit time past
old wounds

errant shifts
to arrive at the place
of my spawning
the dawning
a regressive awakening

forsaking substance
i see the collective episodes
of the years endured
begin to fall away
and the enveloping warmth
of the Sun replete
begins to rapture me
as i allow the letting
of this illusory identity
of how i once defined my self

i now begin to intake
and absorb
the verdant scents
of my holy inner garden
enticing me
as i am reverently approaching
my own presence
my essence
my consummate self

i am barefooted
and my toes become entwined
in the damp soils
of what i thought to be
a forgotten consciousness
a lost knowing
and i begin to glow

i hear sounds about me
within me
attuning itself in concordance
dancing in my heart
playing a tune called bliss
and i know
i have been kissed
by the regality
of that which is sovereign
over all that exists

my loins become incensed
with a primal urging
a needing
to undress
and to express
and my innocent nakedness
stands before the world

my passions begin to unfurl
fulfill themselves
with an incalculable esoteric copulation
and my reason becomes orgasmic
and loses its tethers
to the finite memories
of what i once accepted
defended
as life

i am reflecting my own creational exponential-ness

tears begin to flow
down my cheeks
from my 3rd eye
blinding me
with rivulets of joy
which become streams
which become rivers
before they touch my feet
which now stands
in the Ocean of life

Time freezes
Time ceases
and i am appeased
for now i please myself

for in reflective grandeur
i realize
i am who i have always been

upon the surface of these pristine waters
i look upon my countenance

the glass is no longer darkly
and i thus see
a contextual reflection of me
of self
of God
of Creation
and there is but
a Solitary Tower of Light
enjoining Heaven and Earth
and i am He

measuring things

315 degrees
of this pie of life has been eaten
7 slices
and i am sickened
filled to the point
of regurgitation
but it is that last slice
that will do me nice
to complete me
360 degrees
full circle
a merry go round

i have been on my knees
for aeons
while playing on utterances
prayers
seeking to abate my fears
my tears
but wanting to flow
you know what i mean

of life

Breath

is but a recycled treasure

a gift

countless

given to a Billion years

through countless smiles

countless tears

countless joys

countless fears

and still we hold on

memories faded

almost instantaneously

of that first one

as we souls migrate

to the last one

which will never come

will it ?

the symbiotic nature of nature

the we's

the Trees

the Algae

the me's

the you's

should usher forth a reverence

but we only lament

what seems to be the ending

of a mans dreams

while redeeming life

breath by breath

i smiled at God

and He smiled back

through me

and i felt His glow

warm me

and gratitude adorned my face

as i reflected

on a thing greater

yet as i am

but a breath

of life

"I Am Thankful"

Father,
let me melt into the abysmal arms
of thy grace
for i am thankful

i look about me and i see wonder
and for this gift of sight
i am humbled
and tears moistens my eye
and i am humbled

i feel the beat of your Heart
within mine
and i listen
to the concordant symphony
of life
and conclude reverently
that You and i
are one

the strife and anguish
that challenges my glee
sadly resides in me
but as thy servant James spoke
i count it all joy
so i give my yoke of burden
unto thee

this unceasing breath
that fills my breast
many times goes unnoticed
in my conscious
but i embrace it just the same
with the love of life

yes, i am thankful

the attitude of gratitude
does elude me
many a day
for as a man
i do not always understand
Your ways
but i do remember
what you said
for it forever plays
in my head
that "your Ways are not my Ways"

this does beckon me
to Trust in your judgment
and i am thankful,
for if i had to do it
i would screw it
up

i am thankful for all the challenges
trials
tribulations
you have adorned my path with
for i am the Wiser
the Stronger

the more determined
in my stumbling
my bumbling

it is that darkness
i have learned the nature of Thy Light
and i Fight for it
daily
without fail
within me
and the world about me
I am thankful

this day, my cup is overflowing
for this day i rest in the knowing
that You Father still love me
and i feel this
this existential bliss
this kiss of life
filled with possibilities
for what i may become

so in summing up this brief relief
of what my heart seeks to speak
there is but 3 words
i know you have heard
so many times before
and that is
"I Am Thankful"

I remember in the beginning

i remember in the beginning
i gave you the keys to my heart
and you gave me that of your own
we embraced in the newness
of new love
like there was no tomorrow
just now

in humble reverence
we each proceeded to unlock our treasures
found in each other
the chains that kept that door
secure
in the chamber where
we thought we were safe

time went on
from dawn to dawn
we lived
as if smiles and joy
was all we knew
me and you

we kissed we danced
we shared we dared
to explore
what goodness could possibly be

we knew God was with us
for we trusted thus

it's all possible... isn't it?

it is going on 6 years now
and i am still mal-adjusted

though i do not see your form anymore
i still feel your presence
your persuasion
of my feelings
my thoughts
and my spirit

i still listen for your voice
but i only hear it
when i sit still
and visit the chambers
where memories are stored

the children?
yes, the children
they still feel the anguish
of your departing
our hearts and
our lives were torn apart

sure we had ample warning
you were leaving
but who wanted to listen
or prepare for it
shit, we are still grieving

so what is the resolution
is there a solution
a reconciliation
we are missing here ?

today is another Sunday
feels like any other day
Church has lost its meaning
even though
i did not go then
but just to be there
as you prepared the children . . .

my what special moments
the hustle and bustle
the scurrying around
i mean, just the noise
and excitement

preparing breakfast
the smell of the bacon
the eggs
the biscuits
the hot iron
creasing pants and blouses

will you hurry up in the bathroom
have not heard that plea
in a long, long time

packing the children in the car
the running back in for bibles and such
the fussing
no cussing
the final touch up
the brushing of their hair
on the way out the door

you know,
i ask...
the last time you went out the door
alone
had i known
could i have stopped you

and now i learn
the power of healing was our own
funny the twists it all takes
life that is

we hold to the tales
that we shall meet again some day
but in some way
i feel that you never left
but it would be nice
to see you again
the children would love that too
we miss you much
do such things happen?

it's all possible... isn't it?

i don't want to dance no more

i ask
what sort of God am i
do i truly reign over my life

what dimension does that truism
become valid ?

i have plucked the feather
from a thousand Eagles
along with some Goose down
for comfort
that i may adorn myself daily
as i roll
through this
mucky
murky
sticky
liquid
that adheres to the skin
my skin
my thoughts
of blackness
like the Pitch
the bitch
that it is

perhaps
just maybe
if i put them on right
i to may be able to fly

i doubt it
but it's worth a try

though it did not work yesterday
you know what they say
"today is another day"
the same old shit
it seems to me

so maybe
i ain't that guy
that God they tell me i am
save in that other dimension
that come about
when i sleep
someone please turn the music down
i don't want to dance no more

do you know the way to wonderland ?

you can't blame them
i do understand
been there before

hey man
let's get fukked up
see if we can make it last
just 1 big blast
and maybe we can escape this mess
that tests the very essence
of our soul

i do understand
i have been there before
knocking without cease
on that door
begging
pleading
and needing
some understanding
damn
i was demanding
and no one heard my cries
no one answered that door
so i just turned around
and went and got me 1 more

bag of dope
that i could cope
with the dope and the fukking life gave me
with no soap
to make it slippery enough
to ease on by
and in

and dammit
i still have that same age old question

"Why"

do you know the way to wonderland?

fly anyway, it is a good death . . .

like the Son of Daedalus
i adorned my wings
in hopes to fly away
from the peril about me

i looked to the Great light
i leapt
i soared the skies
seeking my heaven

how lovely
the embracing
of the expansive expressions
of that which my Soul longed for

the Great Sun kissed me
in warmth never felt before
and the door of transition
began to open
allowing me to dream
of what was to come

Icarus was my name
then
and now
i know not
what i have become

my energy began to wane
as i profanely struggled
against life's truth
and my Moon like waxings
melted in the face
of the great truth
and that is
the heat of truth
does bring forth a certain Death

so i like so many others
who vied
have died this day
and this verse i give to you
is my ominous request
speaking through the annals
of an auspicious myth

go my child . . .

fly anyway

it is a good death . . .

his expectations were dying

choking on his dreams
those he was made to swallow
ingest
for life no longer
offered any hope
of resolution

the solutions most good people
once believed in
had faded with the light
as the long night
occupied the lives of men
and the sin of it all
is simply
we have given up

the beliefs once cherished
such as prayers
and other reverent obeisance
offered to the heavens
have been forsaken
for God did not act
as fast as we wished Him to

who are we
that we would dictate
to the prefect
of creation

an arrogant lot
are we not
and like Lot
we had better not
turn around
and look back

our psyches
are under attack
from the impetuous mechanics
of the machine
which is as cold as any steel
and does not feel
for you
nor i

brothers have divorced their empathy
for one another
who wants to be bothered
with having to drag
someone else's burdens
were not our own
heavy enough

shiny big churches
with huge choruses
wearing shiny new robes
and souls with holes
singing hallowed songs
to themselves

is this the same choir
the preacher preached to
and even they could not hear
the word
and the ominous approach
of the Damn Master
as he encroached
upon their lingering heavens

my trusts are unleavened
but my lust is ever rising
cause i just did a trick with
Sista McCleary last night
right after Mrs. Jones done me
there was clearly something wrong

Billy Paul prophesied that
you see
he sang that thang
that song
into reality
and now we are all caught up
wrought up
vexed and hexed up
drowning in that cup
of tears of the soul
or was it the tears of a smile
these false smiles
Smokey spoke of
where is the love ?

Happy New Year

there have been many mountains
and valleys as well
toils woes and anguish
too many to tell
but we made it through

i have questioned my path
in the day, in the night
i have struggled to understand
that final insight
just like you

the world about us
disease, famine war
i have asked, "if this is life?"
what is it good for
and yet we are here

so another year comes
is this but another test
and my only resolution is
may i give life my best
i pray you God to hear me

i have had love and i lost
that a new way may start
and the truth of it all
i still have my heart

so i bow in gratitude
for here i still stand
and perhaps this year
i will understand

that life's beauty is the journey
and the paths that we take
and when it all is over
i pray i am awake

that i may see the sunshine
and realize my sum
and have faith in this year
that the best is yet to come

Happy New Year

Glass Houses

we often go shopping for windows
and Someone's Glass House as well
"DO TELL
what the hell are
you going to do
with that Rock Son
seems like to me
you only need One

yep,
just throw it straight up in the air
and see if you can catch it
and if you are lucky
you won't

and perhaps it will crash
and smash
that delusional reflection of self
you see
and the way you look at me
look at the world
through the windows
of your own Glass House

Home... come

there is a flame
that burns
in the deepest recess of my heart
and it burns for you,
waiting for you
lighting your pathway home

the child within me
sits in solace
quietly praying
for your safe return
that i may hold you again
in the embrace
of the Holy

the Angels dare not make a sound
for the reverence
of this sacred moment
which holds all eternity
calls forth but a word
a voice
only God himself may speak

and we await pensively
for that utterance of praise
when the Bride and her Groom
are reunited
in the chamber of matrimonious union

as my Brother Solomon once said
thy Breast, my Love are Comely
and i long to lay my head
and listen to the Universal rhythms
of thy heartbeat
as it speaks and confirms
the truth of our oneness

images of long ago
sweet memories
still dance
and dominate my thoughts,
for consciousness
of your "here-ness"
is all i desire

so long have i longed
to feel thy gentle touch
upon the skin of my reality
that it may dispel these delusions
yes, delusions i have created
to keep me company,
delusions that you
have never left me

i had to deny this truth
to maintain my sanity

it is not vanity
but my "Vain-ness"
that does adorn the wall of my house,
that which whispers questions
offering a confirmation
while seeking an affirmation
that i do deserve thee

but truth of the Light to be told
"I NEED THEE"
to complete me,
and fulfill the cup of my dreams
that i may drink again
from that fountain of love
born in the Womb of Creation,
in you

i have kept the lantern of hope burning
for surely if i am not diligent
darkness would consume me . . .
again

i abide in this whirlpool of convolution
with my loins afire
with this burning desire
and a relentless passion
that again we will consummate
our union
before the throne
which is seated
in the Garden of the Divine

this is the Sweet Fruit
that of a Soul fulfilled
where the Harvest is never ending

and thy sweet nectar of bliss
shall again drip
from my lips
and you shall feed that need
for me to plant my seed
of the divine

i shall plant them
in the furrows of thy goodness
the "IS"-ness
where the Children of Sovereignty are Born
spawned in spite of
that which comes
to claim the hopes of man

and i a Retired Warrior
now sit in this Silence
listening for your Foot Steps . . .
i know them well

for each foot print of anticipation
is indelibly etched in my heart
as i sit here
on the edges of sunshine
cloaking myself with Dreams
Visions
Prayers

and other Supplications
to Creation
and He who holds all things

i keep this Flame
for i am the "Keeper"
of that "Eternal Light"
within me

and each Heart Beat
each Breath
confirms that it is so
as i await your presence
your return
Home . . . Come

eat one

misplaced words
waiting to be re-discovered
arranged
employing me
to deploy
their power

i sit as a linguistic wannabe craftsman
in an acrostic cerebral solitude
gathering thoughts
that i may assign them
and convey them
in some disconnected hope
for change

the poem is my lifeline

another stanza concludes itself
with no particular determination
it just quits on me

space . . .

begin again . . .

attempting to
recapture the dancing muse
whose syllabic syncopation
teases forth
a delusional mastery
does it all connect ?

i suspect in some realm
there is one at the helm
of this drifting ship
who embraces the Seas
in movements
that appear discordant
but there is a symphony here
that only the attuned ones can hear
can you i am asked

the voice beckons to be heard
there are no words attached
they manifest from the Ju Ju
the beans planted in smiles
eat one

grey days

we sort through clouds
seeking sunshine
employing our light within
seeking passage
to the heavens that we seek

the quest of all souls
i ponder
do we all have
that innate wonder
for things unseen
but remembered
within our divine life seed

the smiles of those
who may not be familiar
it seems as that
of my own
is this another evidence
of oneness
that universal language
we all speak

a slight snicker escapes
my constraints
as i think in lyrics
while humming to some song
i know not

perhaps we can manifest
that light we desire
for it is said

we are Gods

*somewhere within
a distant whispering psyche
speaks of such grandeur
i long to embrace
like a brother i know
but cannot remember
but still he is mine*

*my inner ear twinges
with an expectation
of his voice
of familiarity
that will stir my joy
and infect my expressions
with joy*

*'til then
i sit in this packaged solace
a construct of necessity
and i have weaved this quilt
tightly
and well
for its warmth
though
visceral
is as real as it gets
right now
though i am surrounded
by the embrace
of
grey days*

every day

she sat in her room
almost all alone
just herself
God,
a Muse
and memories
and it was enough

she was not playing house
but playing home
wishing for warm things
the way they use to be

she dressed the dolls
with smiles and love
using big brother's red Magic Markers
to draw hearts on their faces
and any spaces she could find
God smiled too

i could tell you
there was no sunshine in her life
but that would be a lie
for she vied for it each day
when the rains of anguish
did not chase her inside
within herself

but she knew God was there
waiting for her
for He must have been lonely too

when she did go out to play
she did so with an unbridled passion
for she played to forget
the beatings
her Mother endured
from a man
who acted not like her Father

though he was
so long ago
he has been this way
every since he lost his job
and now they had to rob
Peter to pay Paul
when they could find him

and there were the voices inside
that was always waiting for her
in her special hiding place
the place she went
when she did not wish to face
the harshness of the possibilities
that the realities
she now endured
would last forever

whatever . . .

Mommy spent much time alone as well
locked in her room
she never smiled any more
like she used to
when they were a real family

but she, this little girl
found happiness
in those secret places
her own world
where she could dream
as she wished
about whatever she wanted
though she was haunted
by these dreams
that seemed
like they would never come back home

and this is why
she spent so much time in her room
where she could paint the walls with happiness
instead of the gloom
that living was giving to her
every day

disturbing my conversation with my muse ?

he was slamming metaphors of happiness
into his consciousness
hoping to write something beautiful
to no avail

what truly ailed him
was not found in words
for the feeling has yet to manifest
into cognizable words

one could say he was lonely
or confused
but the court crier
thought differently

he surmised
he considered
he pondered
he reflected
he inspected
and no solution was detected
just the absence of all things
of meaning

he visited upon the Book of Faces
there were many
5,000 i think
none whom he knew,
truly

how could he
he did not even know himself
but just the same
it would have to make do
for now

perhaps he would invite a "friend"
to join him
in the meadow of flowers
behind the barn
and they could share a verse or two

he wondered
what would the outcome be
would it be painful
or just another exercise
of less than meaningful words
collected to acknowledge
the accomplishment
of collaboration
betwixt himself
his pen
and the conjurings
he managed

perhaps he would write about the mountain
he could never scale

it is not that he failed
but he never did try
though in his head
all his life he vied
for such feats

many a time he saw himself
at the summit
dammit, who's on the phone now
disturbing my conversation
with my muse ?

did you take the Red Pill or the Blue one ?

a President was killed
shot dead in the head
for all to see
on International TV
we watched
horrified

sure, we cried
because a piece
of the people's hope
died that day
what could one say

we went to sleep
tears staining our dreams
of peace

we believed
what Warren told us
sold us
with no immediate fuss
until years later
when it does not matter
for the agenda
had been served

fast forward
toward
that fateful day
April 4, 1968
when another voice in the Wilderness
that special light for the blind

was snuffed
tough shit they said

did we cry again
sure we did
and we went back to sleep
weeping in our dreams
and Martin's too
of that Mountain Top
which began to melt
for the vision of the people
became lowly
slowly
knowingly
by those who keep their fingers
on the buttons
your buttons
my buttons
and the buttons
of the children to come
a now unquantified sum
of misery and suffering
with no KY Jelly to ease the pain
no buffering

silence one voice . . . silence many

yeah, they experimenting
concocting ideas
marinating them
fermenting them
until the spirits are ready
to inebriate our wills

by way of the information actions
the factions feed us
and the tidbits of lies spilled
while we be chillin'
and illin just like Mr. Little spoke of

you see
they slipped on by
you and me
Humanity
in February
of that year 1965
while we were
shucking and jiving
being cool
in 65 an' beyond
we thought
but "Red" knew
that you were sleep
and when he woke up
he spoke on it
gave us the 411
the dope
to smoke on it

shit
did we even hear it
the words
the message
or are we celebrating the messenger
listen as "X" speaks
it is a factor
but first
i know, i know

you must finish that Tweet
that Text
what's next ?

Tupac ?
yeah he's gone too
but his words live on
or do they
what do you say
has your soul spoke its truth
today

we must continually
in the spirits of our ancestors
convey
this truth

Our youth are at risk
as are we
and this applies not to a "Just Us",
but to humanity
from Syria to Bosnia
Sierra Leone to your home
Afghanistan to your land
from L.A. to your way
from Brownsville to your village
just like yesterday
today
and tomorrow

if we don't wake up
get up
and cease this spillage
of the people's blood

and tears
while our fears
are being exploited
deployed in Detroit
and anywhere
it serves the purpose
of those
who offer no service
to humanity
save the insanity
that continues this venue
of disconnectedness
amongst each other
my Sisters and my Brothers

but in the meantime
i have
a question for ya . . .
did you take the Red Pill or the Blue one ?

Trinity

I know why you're here, Neo. I know what you've been doing... why you hardly sleep, why you live alone, and why night after night, you sit by your computer. You're looking for him. I know because I was once looking for the same thing. And when he found me, he told me I wasn't really looking for him. I was looking for an answer. It's the question that drives us, Neo. It's the question that brought you here. You know the question, just as I did.

Neo
What is the Matrix?

Trinity

The answer is out there, Neo, and it's looking for you, and it will find you if you want it to.

happily here after

hypocrites in the woodshed

gathering chips and shit

trying to build Castles

with waste

just like their cousins

over yonder

who build mountains

out of mole hills

i wonder

where do such dreams

come from ?

were their parents

errant

in the assertions as well ?

always attempting to dispel

cast to hell

the pre-emptive

common sense

and decency

while conjuring

visceral fancies

i be dandy

in lieu

of honesty

honestly, will we endure

this coming shift

of Creation's

relations

to our Consciousness

or will we just

go back to the woodshed

and practice building Castles

that can not stand

and perhaps live

happily here after

Daydreaming again

she wore a Kama Sutra smile
that enticed me to think only
of the possibilities

yes, i was intrigued
indeed
to step off that precipice
of wonder
no wonder i am in a daze
and the haze of her persona
her aura
has me blinded

there was a scent
of her womanhood
lingering in the air
that transcended my logic
and my mind immediately raced
and embraced her
and on the tip of my tongue
i could taste her
damn she was sweet

my feet were immobilized
and i realized
it did not matter
whether my eyes
were open
or closed
i suppose
i belonged to her now

and somehow
she had captured my thought
my attention
not to mention
my time,
yes, this dime piece
made me grab my peace
and saddle my horse
for the ride
and there was no hiding
my arousal

any damn one could see
what she had done
and was doing
to me

damn
i was losing my sanity
but that is OK
cause i am having a ball

my heart was doing strange things
making strange noises
as it rose to my throat
choking off my breath
damn
did i say she was fine
yes, she had my mind
all F'ed up

it was not that i had a choice here
for when she spoke
her voice made me melt
and i felt
the animals of lust
running though my blood
my veins
this is insane

i was being consumed
with want
desire
and this fire inside
defied
all will
and though i was stilled
my thoughts were ill
as i could only see myself
spilling myself
planting seed indeed
in the furrows
of her holy garden

then i heard a voice
ardently speaking to me
waking me
saying to me
"excuse me Sir . . you are next ?"
yes, i was
Daydreaming again

Flowers in the Wind

like flowers in the wind
we stand upon the Mountainside
witnessing a grandeur replete

with such presence
can not we help
but lend our fragrance
unto life

let my petals be plucked
and cast to the world
that all may know
that i have been

but . . .
like a flower in the wind

inspired by way of a Note from Lins . . . .
much love dear friend . . .

here on the ground

we live in an age of limitation
voluntarily clipping our own wings
daily
yet . . .
we dream of flying
which now resides
in the shadows that haunts us
as memories
of our greater selves

we were fashioned of that ilk you know
we are but mini-Gods
who have chosen to live
or die
in perceptible slowness
vibrating our magnificence
in secret
that no one may know

our souls struggle
against our consciousness
as we abate
to relate
to the sedated ones
fixated on belonging
i think

don't blink
for life will pass you by
again
in this eternal blossom
which holds to no end

cycles are but that
redundant passes
of that which has been
but we like games
don't we

like Monopoly
we live for that passing of "GO"
to be temporarily sated
with a mere $200.00
you know

i smile at myself
and the me i see in you
as we acquiesce to some unknown belief
and convince ourselves
it is righteous
to stay . . .
here on the ground

Don't you ?

Them old Oak Trees of the South wood
Expressed an almost forgotten familiarity
Their statuesque presence looming
Sketching outlines in the skies above
As i looked up

Looking down
You could see their deciduous brethren
Gathered at their feet, mostly
But some of the Ancients
Did challenge their girth

Barren because the Winter took notice
Leaves fallen upon the earth
You could smell the composting of the Oak
As it continued its journey to nurture
And feed the life to come

The background skies just adorned them
In the allowing of their interruptive limbs
To their own expanse and command of what we see
All was peaceful, and none held angst
About another

The Brother of mine, Wind
Still danced, still pranced
Without much resistance
There was nothing really to do
But visit his old friends
And remind them of their symbiosis
For each were born, all were born
With gnosis, as are we

We have forgotten the purpose of the way
Yet each day we awaken and trek forward i think
But then again, what do i know
Save that all rivers flow to Oceans
Eventually, don't they ?

The Sun was seeing what i was, wasn't it
And so much more i am sure
For when i act as a Sun, i do
I thought you knew
Don't you ?

fractured disconnectedness . . .

we deliberately
tender our words
that we not be ostracized
from that fake
"Circle of Acceptance"

those who would be a Warrior
dull their swords
and reluctantly
take the edge off
of their convictions
only to feel
the Soulful constrictions
that comes about
when we live
un-actualized
to our Sacred, Instinctive Truths

our personal political maneuverings
guarantees not a solace
we all have longed for
and we curse the landscape
the garden
that nurtures
these seeds of our errancies
we have voluntarily sown

i always ask
had i have known . . . would i

no sense in lying
nor denying
for i chose to defy
my higher self
while edifying delusions
of self

eeeerrrrr . . .
now what was i saying here ?

my deliberate confusion
will not save me
my indifference
will not bathe me
absolve me
redeem me
nor blind me
for i still do see
myself

not a pretty picture
even when i close my eyes
and surmise
about change

and we are all too willing
to settle for the
loose change
with our deranged reason
but there is no appeasing
that reality
is it

every morning
every dawn
we must awaken
to face
that same person
who went to sleep last night
with their tasks undone

and we know today
will be much of the same
don't we

funny how everyone
can see you for who and what
you are
and you do too
don't you
but will you
walk that reconciliatory path
and be ..
yes i said "BE"
without the fractured disconnectedness . . .
of your self
your true self

the health of civilization
is dependant on you
so what you gonna do ?

Heaven again

i took money
i took the toaster
i got laid

me, i took the trip
the all expense
never to be paid vacation
around the flag pole
and then they stuck
it up my azz
with the 24.99% APR

what did you take
in lieu of
your divinity
where peace of mind
and serenity
were once ours

guess i'll buy a lottery ticket
and if i win
it's on
Heaven again

do we understand

do we really even understand
what is happening here
in Amerikka
the land . . . of the FREE ?
do we really understand my friend
how you and me
are gonna be
if we don't awaken

the forsaken amongst us
our people
are being displaced
with no place
to lay their head
no bed
but that of a park bench
while the stench
of the streets of the filth
of our indifference
permeates our own souls
do we understand
tell me my brother
do we understand

yes the children
what about the children
those of the lost

who but we all
yes "WE" all
will pay this cost
as our humanity is being tried
no, it can't be denied
yes they have lied
and will continue
the venue
as long as we let them
do we understand

do we understand
the sickness
and disease
please tell me
you feel me
and you are with me
for we must do something
don't we?
please tell me you understand

people, families, communities
falling
as the banks are calling in
the inflated interest loans
that should have never been
what a sin

and if they don't get it
your own government will
as they foreclose
for taxes
on those who cannot keep up
they can kiss my axes

no taxation without representation
was once the cry of the land
and i cannot
but my brother
tell me
please tell me you understand

a land of plenty
for a few
do really like this New day
new way of living
what lessons are we giving
our children
please tell me you understand

please tell me you understand

inspired via Adrian Hall sharing with me a Brian O'Neal Video

Damn Muses... gotta love them

i have taken a seat beside the waters
and i listen to the babble
of the babbling brook
while looking upon the reflective rivulets
as my life streams by

the superfluous needs are evident
for my tears are flowing to join the run
the journey
to the ocean
where perhaps meaning may be lacking
but the embrace is calming

the questions of life
i have let go
and my frustrative heart vacated as well

yes, tired is an understatement
life never did offer a full stomach
in my brief stay here
all the meals
were but a temporary cessation
to what angst ?
i cannot tell
for all i know is the emptiness

oh sure, like most of us
i vied for happiness
cried as well

and as far as i can tell
it is but a state of mind
until you find something else to focus on
and then . . .
yes . . . and then it is gone
vanishes in the ether

and neither way
whether i am Yinging
or i am Yanging
can i in permanence
tether its attributes
to my nonplussed Soul

we speak such lies in word
like Namaste'
do you have a mirror
so that i can peer
through that looking glass
the one where you see God ?
not just feel Him
for feelings are but a tease

i wish to be blinded like Tommy
by the Light
and have Elton sing
my Wizard Song
and i will Hum along
while sitting by this babbling Brook
who took time
to dictate this Poem

Damn Muses . . gotta love them

Grandma says

be mindful

of the words of the Wolf

for they will beguile

and seduce your mind

that is what happened to me

it all started one lonely afternoon

when i heard this charming voice

telling me

he

could fill my emptiness

and look at me now

somehow

i have lost my way

because of all those sweet things

that beguiling Wolf did say

his words were sweet

and complete

and made me dream

of things i have long forgotten

and before i knew it

i was his begotten

oh that sweet voiced wolf

yet

i have no regrets

and every time

i think of that beguiling Wolf

i smile

this is what Grandma says . . .

est tempus

in the quiet of night
you came to my rest
a place of quiet solace
when silence
transmuted me to purpose

you whispered in my ear
est tempus
it is time
mea filius vos requiruntur
my son you are required
hic in nunc
here in the now

my consciousnes rose to greet
and feel the kiss of your words
syllable by syllable
upon my longings
for i knew of this coming
of your radiance,
the magnificence
of you heavenly confluence
with my soul

i was erect with temptation
for a certain congruence
of our union
had to be

i wanted to re-enter
your womb
where my spawning took place
a dawning of something
beyond the ultimate
as held in the eyes of men

a quixotic rhythmn took hold
laid seige
to my hopes
and waste them upon the abyss
where there is naught but death
and nothingness
for this time was definitively
pre-eminent

my own tongue was loosed
and the delusion of my speech
that at one time i thought
to have made sense
was clarified
and made anew and straight

a new tongue became known
unto me
so i babble no more
for the world of illusion

the gutteral utterances ushered forth
appeared as an ectopic light
resonating with utopic wonder
revealing Thothian like angles
opening unworn pathways
that i may cross the Fourth safely

and i arose
displaying an actualized splendour
i always had known was mine

i watched at the gate of observation
as my vessel arose
to perform the duty at hand
and transport my essence
to that portal
for the final fare had been exacted

and i knew
with a certainty that could never be challenged
by the empiracy
and that is simply as simply can get

est tempus

"i lay down my life that i may pick it up again, for i have the power to do so"

damaged goods

i am jaded and scarred
but i pray not that i remain calloused
for i have known love before

she visited upon me
one fair day
and my heart embraced her

i have looked upon the world
with a jaundiced eye
for the movement about me
expressed itself
with undue
perhaps due
pains
woes
anger
discordance
and i saw
nor felt
no reason
to dance

how my soul longs
for the faint memories
of times
that must have been
for i ache
for goodness
for love

i at times dwell betwixt
dimensions
with a dissension
from what is sold to me
as reality
and my angst grows
as my temperance wanes
for the inane claim
that this is all there is

what is my business here
this journey
where fear promulgates
upon the souls and psyches
of our brethren

the doubt we embody
that speaks lies
defying Eden
while we offer hope
and pleading
to Source
within
and without

my sarcasm
is ever vigilant
seeking to cast dispersion
upon that we see as but
experiential
never quite grasping
the Now
and the potential we possess
to alter how we address

life

we see too many lines
and not the blending
take notice to our differences
the Criers cry
oh my
who trained these vagrant souls
the Dogs
to the Water Hydrants of Life

piss on me
leave and indelible stain
and scent
of waste
and we shall build upon it

i seek the Flowers and Butterflies
Pain knows me well
but who shall it be left
to tell the Children

will we leave a legacy
written in books
that the illiterate ones
may look at the pictures
smiling faces
with desolate backgrounds
and colors of light
laced through
the darkness

i write letters, words
upon soiled sheets of paper

hoping the new messages are seen
some may ingest them
who amongst us quest for this as well
please tell me

new spirits maybe
are we just re-cloaking the lies
that we may get along
through another errant millennium

from drugs of Doctrine
to drugs of Delusion
to Xanax
and broken dreams
that were never tethered
nor anchored
nor rooted
in the soils of "Is"-ness
what business is it of ours
of yours

page #'s flying by
emoting words and thoughts
catalogued for future use
but are we truly blinded
or just faking it

who will filter what
the higher mind of us
should ingest ?
before the letting
of the final drop of blood
that we may be saved
from ourselves

with all these questions abound
i ask around town
and in the Village
there are Vendors
who lay claim
that they have the map

have you visited?
No is the reply
but i have it on good authority
that this is the true way
so i have been told

let us build another steeple
in the quicksands of time
and sacrifice our convictions
upon the fair grasses
that the sheeple may eat

we will cast from us
the ones we label derilictionous
for they may divert
our own purpose
of control
of the masses of souls
and people will look
seek
and peek
under the skirts
of our pretty dresses of program

we most certainly
do not wish them to see their reflections
do we

for then they would see
a greater truth
that they are powerful
and divine
and truly not
the damaged goods
we have preached
all these years

and should they cry again
they will vie again
as their Soul matter is rinsed
cleansed again
and we all will see
the "I" in me
is that of a truth
of certainty
when we lay down our lives
and die again
forsaking
these man-made crosses
we bear

with a tear and a smile
rejecting the illusions
homemade delusions
that we are vile
representations of that
which is perfect
the prefect
of the goodness
and the damaged goods

Half Moon Light, Half Moon Dark

I stand in the not so silent night
Contemplating the resonating of life about me
And me is semi-absent form this consciousness
What a mess
The test to find ones way
Out of their own convolutions created
Never to be abated perhaps

Half Moon Light, Half Moon Dark

But we must believe
So they tell us
Or we will never achieve
What I may ask

Half Moon Light, Half Moon Dark

The task at hand always
In all ways
In all the days
Is to find our way
Through our own wilderness

Half Moon Light, Half Moon Dark

My mind stirs and picks at things
Singing songs I have forgotten
To annoy me
Or incite me
To further the quest of being free

Half Moon Light, Half Moon Dark

The body has need of things
But there is this thing inside of me
That cares not about such things
For I am enjoying just the "being"-ness of things

Half Moon Light, Half Moon Dark

I cling to the nothingness
In my feeble attempts to make it something-ness
Another fine mess William
For thy inquisitiveness
Comes with a payload of reservations
Doubts and Fears abound
And they never flee
At the sound of my feeble
Soul Blowing of what I claim certain
And certainly I will never overcome
That which is the ultimate validity

Half Moon Light, Half Moon Dark

The moon peaks through the clouded heavens
Half Moon Light, Half Moon Dark
There is a distant train whose whistle is blowing
For those who seek the knowing
To awaken
From their soon to be forsaken journey
And still the resonant "I" in me
Wants of things

Half Moon Light, Half Moon Dark

*And the equation that fulfills itself
Has cosigned to imbalance
So it seems
Yet in the dreams
I am whole, wholly
Even in my folly*

Half Moon Light, Half Moon Dark

*Am I the light
Or the dark
Or a contextual representation of the complete*

Half Moon Light, Half Moon Dark

*I must ask again
Am I ?
Half Moon Light, Half Moon Dark*

i am a Souldier

i am a Souldier
in the Community
the Community of Humanity
i bring the word of truth
based upon my love to serve

i am a Souldier
in my Community
i come to you my Brother
my Sister
and i give you my heart
for i am a Souldier

i draw out my sword
that i might smite the darkness
that creeps in our realm
of goodness
by way of my word
my intent
and as i said
my love

for i am a Souldier

dancing with delusional libidos

it was a dismal time
upon the map
of man's evolution

the skies of hope were bleak
and sunshine was doled out
rationed
to those who fashioned
to accept the new way of delusions

the rain was not purple
and there were no princes
nor princesses

there were just children of humanity
scratching the earth surface
of their consciousness
seeking grubs of understanding
to sustain their lives
with any
life giving
rife giving
substance
they could uncover

bias amongst each other
had become an accepted way
they were created in stride
that men's true love
for one another
would not have to be confronted
for that would usher forth

self-judgment
and none wanted to be condemned

diversionary tactics

we redress old truths
with new lies
and our eyes behold
pretty delusions
we hold to our hearts
while hoping for
fanciful epiphanies
to deliver us

we do this
in relationship
government
self
claiming
our ship
was meant
to sail
without fail
to that dry dock
to claim our wealth
for which
we are not even prepared

we are still anchored
in the mud
of the bay
hoping
trusting
for some Coast Guard

to rescue us
with the deliverance
of that winning Lottery Ticket
that we may run
from our own shadows

our souls are bared
that the anguish of truth
would have its way
as we seek to resurrect our nights
to become some day
a magic
a blessing
are we testing God
or some other idyllic
acrylic surreality

so i retire myself
and seek a "Good Book"
hoping to get a good look
at the Rook
who shall save me
and Castle me
but i usually wind up
boxed in a corner
with my brother Jack
eating some more damn
Curds and Whey
Horner that is
who also danced

but that's another nursery rhyme

divine expression

a dark spirit came upon me . . . man
one not common
in the realm
of my understanding

it affected
and thus infected me,
causing me to vie
and rise up against my brother
and let his blood
upon the soil
of our blessings

i shall call her name . .
"en~vy"
for she is in me
and has found a home
in this, my private eternity

when will i be loosed

i was stripped of my honor
and cast to an unknown wilderness
and destined to know of a woman
who was not of my rib

we made a sort of
discordant conjugal music
chorused with tongues
that babbled
in non-symphonious tones
ushering forth and eschewed view

of my distant fading memories
of my smiles and
of Eden
a place where Abel was able
to outshine me
in the eyes of that Entity
which Lorded over us
with enmity

was this seed of tortuous expression
the fault of my Mother ?
or is some other generational curse
exacting such a suffering
in my crooked walk

was it the lack of forthrightness
of my "Earthly Seed Bearer",
Adam
who is the progenitor
of my woes . . .
who knows

my feet, my toes,
oh how they do miss
the damp verdant laden soils
of that garden,
that which my ardent heart
still yet dreams of

i vie for a "Celestial Forgiveness"
that will allow me to return,
if but for a "Stilled" visit
in Time's spatial illusion

a delusion will do . . . for now

i yearn to once again
taste the sweet fruit
of the labor of my hands
as the sweat of my brow
nurtures the expectations
of a bountiful harvest

but . . . what was i given
to take with me
in my banishment ?

Prayers and Faith ?

who is it that shall
sequester my earnest requests
for a reprieve
from this cloak of disdain
and despair
i must wear ?

and in a certain knowing
i still am sowing
seeds on hope
as i cope
with this doom filled
looming
dichotomous reality
betwixt a "Good"
and an "Evil"
that manifests

as a test
for all souls
who toil against their reason

none of it makes for
a reasonable defense
that offers a satiable recompense

so i simply speak
in the same voice
of First Father
"Let their be Light"
and i brightly shine
for that seed still resides
within me

i am the Garden
i am the Gardener
which i seek

and all that is thine
is mine
for "I AM" of THEE

i am an unquantified incalculable expression
of the Divine

Faith...

the Cock crew
the Crow caws
Soul falls
Man Calls
out

while housed in this vessel
we wrestle with self
grabbing for strings
to hold on to things
to secure bodies
but bodies does not
secure
that which has not
a home here

the Sun rises
we criticize
our eyes
still see that glint of wonder

light filters through
transmutes
what's within you
and we pull the curtain shut
for we are not ready
are we ?

and the Cock still
does what he does
all through the night now
and the quandary still prevails

what ails man
that he can not find peace
will the search ever cease
for that which is everlasting

we fast
we pray
we give
we say
help me
in many languages
a mixture of joy
of hope
of anguish

souls being tried
vying
lying
crying
dying
where do they go ?

we sow seeds
perform good deeds
trying to balance a "Karma"
Ma never told me about that

the fruit of the spoils
of the sacrifice
escapes my reason
for its sweetness
is but a season
of finite pleasing
and the Gods are teasing us
yet they tell us to trust

all about me
is suffering
and you say
it is perspective.
and that soul in me
laughs
in a most sarcastic voice
and you speak to me
of the choice
of free will

the shrill and the jester
scream and dance
i hear the dichotomous symphony
of life revisited again
reminding me
of the perils of a man
who is filled with questions

self becomes the enemy
the friend
all housed in that vessel
where the eternal like wrestling match
has no time outs
except when i

deliberately delude myself
or seclude my self
in the darkness
which runs and hides from me
offering me not any lasting solace

and still those damn birds
i hear them every dawn
and all day long
reminding me
of what we mourn for
the answering of the prayer for
a better life
where there is a peace
without cease

and still yet
the Cock crew
the Crow caws
Soul falls
Man Calls
out

Faith . . .

of things in a frame

the picture frames hung upon the walls
of my house
in an ambient
yet reverent silence
adorning my home
with a warmth of memories

and there were some
sitting on Coffee tables and such
some were ornate
others plain
but all placed where
there
as a reminder
of this path i have walked
at some time ago
into my "Now"

i sit and revisit
thoughts, smiles and tears
i had let ease into
a state of distant embrace
where these memories had been bedded
embedded into my character
shaping me
molding me
yet still holding me
in a weathered tethered web

that could not
would not
let go

there were pictures
of my children
friends, acquaintances
sisters and brothers
my Father and Mother
and grandchildren too
and many other souls
i at one time knew

and though i was somewhat cognizant
of the people
who adorned this steeple
where my life's alter resided
which coincided in my now
there were the times
that somehow
escaped me
and left me
to become some sort of history
reminding me
of who i used to be

i look at the holders of these memories
and each perhaps had a meaning
some uplifting
some gleaning me
from my hull of self

i look at these frames
who embrace the names
of the times
in a land of rhymes
the ones i loved
and love still

yes, these frames
embrace that part of me
i no longer face
a part of me
i had long put away
just for this day
that i may reflect
while looking
on the meaning
of things in a frame

Frames
sometimes a thought
sometimes a word
sometimes a taste
sometimes a smell
sometime a touch
but always a feeling

in flight . . . and the music played

he closed his eyes
just after twilight
and rode his dreams
towards death
senses enlivened
seeking peace

when he arrived
at the gate
it was chained and locked
and death defied him
once more

he knew
in some uncanny way
that he had to find a way
to cross over
to the other side
for this is the life
the one he was stuck in
he was called upon
to lay down

and the music played

if there was to be change
then all had to change
no remnants of memory
could be held on to

and all the nuances of past pretense
past character
had to be removed
he needed more
than absolution
and this was the solution
the holy revealed unto him

and the music played

he unmounted his steed
and stood by the gate
pondering
wondering
about this plight
this night
and the locked gate
which he had given flight
to only arrive
and be refused entry

and the music played

and gently
he began to weep
and the tears flowed
from his sleep
into his nightmares
and upon his feathered pillow
only to touch again
the resonance of his awareness
in this dream

and the music played

there were shadows
and it seemed
that he was existing
listing
betwixt the two dimensions
for most men's realities
and there hapless actualities
created when one seek to escape
as he did
when he mounted
his steed
in search of the need
he thought he needed
only to find the gate locked
as he did every night
in his flight
towards death

and the music played

so they say

he had no true and devoted friends
just acquaintances
who painted faces
upon themselves
that they may pass by
unnoticed

no one wanted people to see them
as they truly are
so they hid
in shadowed corners
and behind pretty masks
fearing to be asked
to come to the real party
life

we all have endured
that is for sure
so much we did not agree with
haven't we

we all have cursed ourselves
at one time or another
for going along
with the plan
the song
as interpreted
by others
smothering our own
creative intuitions

gathering names

to complete the picture
create the vision
that says we belong
to something

i'll be your friend
what does that mean ?
i query myself far too much
i thought
but . . .
better me than them
i reasoned
with the devil
and he smiled
and complimented me
he said i reminded me of his son
no one never told us
that the devil had children
but now that i think about it
hhhhhhhhmmmmmmmmmm
i know of plenty of folks
who have given me
hell in my life

perhaps it was all in innocence
and they were just inviting me
to their home
for a visit
or sleep over

something about eternity
moves me
and another plateau
of deductive logics

invade my considerations
and all i can do is smile
in lieu of another
empty prayer
that i hear
but do not believe in
my self

do you believe in your self ?
which one may i ask
the one behind the mask
or . . .

well any way
as we meandered down
the multi colored brick road
we surmised it must have been
the remnants of that Lysergic Acid
that tainted our Chromosomes
cause this . . . life
is one "Hell" of a trip
oooopppppss
i meant it is "Heavenly"
forgive me Lorde
and thank you for the blessings
and the bile that goes along with it

i know you have a purpose
"for the Bible told me so"
or was it that guy with the choking white collar
who hollers at us
every Sunday or so
until he is red in the face

i do like the way the veins
pop out his head
do you think God will prevent him
from exploding
just a thought

so this soul based banter i am having
anything viable ?
i do this for me
my best friend
who hides behind the mask
and hides in shadows
for that damn light
is scary
how can it be so special
when so many people have one
so they say

~ * ~ the Jester ~ * ~

I am but a fool in his folly.
I know not of these affairs of men . . .
They are too High Minded for me!

Once upon a time, there was a Wonderful and Magical Kingdom. Like any other Kingdom, there was a King, a Queen, a Prince, a Princess, a Wizard and the Court Jester. The Kingdom like all the other Magical Kingdoms of time, lived in peace. The subjects were a happy people, and the children played joyfully in the fields and gardens. The Sun shined by day, and the Moon by night.

There were no worries anywhere to be found. All the lands and people lived together in love and bliss. All of the people from the King to the Blacksmith performed their daily tasks without any complaints. The King ruled, the Queen advised the King and did Queenly things. The Princess and the Prince embraced life for the good. The Wizard wizarded, and the Jester made all the Kingdom laugh. He entertained the people of the kingdom as he often went amongst them on a visit. He especially had an affinity for Children, and he loved them very much. The Children loved him also for Who and As he was, for he was always happy. This was really a "Story Book" Land!

One day a small child asked him, the Jester . . . "Why are you always so happy?" . . . and the Jester replied . . . "I am but a fool in his folly. I know not of these affairs of men . . . They are too High Minded for me!"

As the people of the Kingdom lived in peace for many years, the word spread to other lands about this Magical place.

We all know that sooner or later . . .

One day a visiting Caravan came upon the Kingdom. In the Caravan were Traders and Wise Men, Magicians and Medicine Men, They were all awed that such a beautiful place existed. They all loved it so much that they desired to find the reason or secret of how this could be, for this was highly unusual and uncommon.

They first went to the King and Queen and inquired. The answer they received was really no answer at all. All the Royal Court could tell them that it was always this way as long as they could remember. Then they approached the Wizard . . . and all he could say was that it was a magic beyond his power and understanding. Then they went amongst the village and questioned the people, but they had no reasonable response either. . . then there was the Child. The child told them, they should ask the Jester! Now this was an unusual approach, for all knew that Jesters were Jokers, and Jokers were Fools, and Fools were Jesters. So, what kind of answer could they possibly expect of a Jester? But at this time what did they have to lose . . . for there was something beautiful in this Kingdom and they had to possess it!

So they caught up with the Jester and proceeded to question him about every aspect of the Kingdom for hours on end. The Jester listened patiently to their inquiries until the visitors had finally exhausted themselves. Then the Jester stood and spun around in a circle making Jest, doing what Jesters do. . . and he replied . . . "I am but a fool in his folly. I know not of these affairs of men . . . They are too High Minded for me!" They all quizzically looked at each other somewhat irritated and puzzled at the same time. Then the Jester smiled broadly at them until they smiled back at him, and then he said again . . . "I am but a fool in his folly. I know not of these affairs of men . . . They are too High Minded for me!"

. . . but this I do know . . .

As the Sun embraces the Earth and blessed the flowers and gardens with it's smile, they smile back at him. As the Moon caresses the night , the evening tide undulates to and fro and thus caresses the lands and nourishes it's thirst. As the hands of the people massage and caress the soil of the earth with attentive care, she yields her bounty that our tables may be always full. As the North Wind blows it's gentle breezes across our brow, thereby removing our sweat as we toil in the gardens, we are thankful.

Though I do not care to know the ways of man, the ways of God are sufficient for me. So, I smile and smiles come back . . . I caress others with a smile, embrace or a kind word, and I myself am soothed. When I lend my hand to another it comes back full. And as I sigh, as I often do each day, I offer my breath to God giving Him my thankfulness for His Perfect Creation.

So I say this . . . I humbly submit to you that . . . "I am but a fool in his folly. I know not of these affairs of men . . . They are too High Minded for me!"

Poets... know that we are the enchanting magicians that nourishes the seeds of dreams and thoughts... it is our words that entice the hearts and minds of others to believe there is something grand about the possibilities that life has to offer and our words tease it forth into action... for you are the Poet, the Writer to whom the Gift of Words has been entrusted.

~ William S. Peters, Sr. ~

Epilogue

a few words from . . . *B*ill

I am thankful . . .

Many times in our lives we are faced with challenges. I think none of us have not at one time or another voiced the infamous question of "why me?". Perhaps there are answers that are absolute. Perhaps these answers we cling to for our peace of mind are but our own means of mitigating through this life journey the best way we can. Either way, it is what it is.

When it is all said and done, i have found that my perspective on Life's *Things* and *Circumstances* are maybe all that i can control. Thus i have adopted an attitude of gratitude and my life has become so much more empowered and enriched.

When i look about me, i have the choice of focusing my attention on energies which in turn drain me or . . . empower me. Gratitude and Thankfulness most certainly wins out each and every time. There are so many things to be grateful for, starting with each Breath and every Heartbeat. I am also grateful for my Family . . . which is every one of you. I am grateful for every experience i have had, to include those once perceived as Good and those i thought to be Negative. I have come to the simple realization that every experience of my life is capable of rendering a lesson . . .some profound . . . and some very subtle, but all are significant at some level. In the end, i think that all the things i once looked upon as mistakes or wrong turns upon my Life Path, were not so. It is those very perceived wrong turns which has delivered me to this *Here*, this *Now,* where i am . . . and for that . . . i am thankful.

'just bill'

William S. Peters, Sr.
www.iamjustbill.com

Janet P. Caldwell is a Prolific and sometimes Eclectic Writer and Poet. She has published two Books thus far, "5 degrees to separation" (2003) and "Passages" (2012). Janet also held her own Byline in a Print Newspaper. Her work is featured in countless magazines as a Free Lance Writer and Poet around the Globe. Her work in Poetry is included in many Collections and Anthologies. Her writing career spans some 30 + years. She is currently working on her third book due in early Spring of 2013.

Janet is a very busy and powerful modern age woman. She is the Chief Executive Officer for Inner Child Enterprises which includes the position of Managing Editor for Inner Child Magazine, Program Director for the Inner Child Radio Network, Administrator of Production and Project Manager for Inner Child Press and Chief Administrator for The Inner Child Social Network.

Janet has a Soul of Gold and is quick to volunteer to assist others without hesitation when called upon to serve humanity. She is a cherished soul by all that know her and have had the opportunity to converse with her and call her friend.

To read more about Janet and her work go to . . .

www.janetcaldwell.com

a few words from . . . Janet P. Caldwell

As one who knows Bill, on many levels, I am honored to be the Project Manager of this book of Spiritually Divine and Enlightened messages, brought to us in the form of Poetry and Prose. The thought provoking questions and endless answers he addresses appears to come from a Higher Source and makes a way for one's own Self Empowerment. As we all know, when one has an opportunity to look at oneself, we are given the ability to go within and recall our own Truth. Finally, through Bill's work we realize that we are not alone in our reservations and / or queries pertaining Dogma and the assigned "Life Purpose" that has been passed down to us for aeons.

Bill has a way to give us, the reader, the ability to think for ourselves and to share in the Brilliance of Wisdom and Knowledge that we all possess. This flows easily from this book into our Inner-Being; based on an infusion of love and understanding. Line by line, we are sated. 'He that hath an ear, let him hear'.

The title itself speaks volumes to the Man and who he is. The Vine as Bill alludes to here is Fruit Bearing and produces such fruit that can be rendered into an inebriating elixir for our Souls. Bill is truly a Keeper of such. He is true to the Title as he Tenderly and Generously cares for his Global Family by way of not only his writing but his life work. He has also been referred to as a Gentle Gardener tending to the seeds he has planted until they reach maturity and Fruition. This is a man of integrity who walks the walk. His Public and private Persona is Loving, Highly Conscious and Gifted. He is truly a blessing to all who know him and much more.

The poems / prose within these pages are Love Expressions and will uplift and stimulate you in every way, every day. Please share in His Journey as you find reflections of yourself in this Powerful Vine Keeper, Mr. William S. Peters, Sr.

Janet P. Caldwell

Author
5 Degrees to Separation
Passages
Chief Administrator Inner Child

Shareef Abdur-Rasheed, AKA, Zakir Flo was born and raised in Brooklyn, New York. His education includes Brooklyn College, Suffolk County Community Colleg and Makkah, Saudi Arabia. He is a Veteran of the Viet Nam era, where in 1969 he reverted to his now reverently embraced Islamic Faith. He is very active in the Islamic community and beyond with his teachings, activism and his humanity.

Brother Shareef has led quite a storied life and has been exposed to and broken bread and communed with many other Artists, Musicians, Activists and Social Luminaries such as The Reverend Al Sharton, Sulaiman El Hadi and Jalal Mansor Nurradin from the original "Last Poets" and many, many others. He himself is an avid Percussionist and has a great passion for the Congas and Timbales. He is a great lover of Afro Cubano, Latin Jazz and Salsa. Throughout his childhood, his Father has exposed him through many of the Jazz greats who have been through New York, and you know this list is far too extensive to mention.

Shareef's spiritual expression comes through the persona of "Zakir Flo". Zakir is Arabic for "To remind". Never silent, Shareef Abdur-Rasheed is always dropping science, love, consciousness and signs of the time in rhyme.

Shareef is the Patriarch of the Abdur-Rasheed Family with 9 Children (6 Sons and 3 Daughters) and 41 Grandchildren (24 Boys and 17 Girls).

For more information about Shareef, visit his personal FaceBook Page at :

http://www.facebook.com/shareef.abdurrasheed1

a few words from . . . Shareef Abdur ~ Rasheed

My brother William (Bill) Peters is a blessing to the world as an artist of great passion and conviction coupled with immense talent and creativity! He has spent a great portion of his life expressing his art through the "eye of his pen" crying blessed ink devoted to touch lives with introspective thought laced with profound "Spiritual Flavor" !! It is an honor as a fellow artist and brother human to not only give "Bill " an endorsement for this new work and his latest of 17 books published but it is a "Duty" to inform the world that a creative force is among us pouring gallons of "Poetic Nectar" in the collective "PunchBowl"!!

Much love, respect and blessings!!

Shareef Abdur-Rasheed

Regina Ann is in a very real sense a Renaissance Woman. Along her path she has delved into a wide array of opportunities. The common threads binding all that she does is empowerment, healing and love. She is a Life Transformation Coach, a Usui Reiki Master Practitioner and Teacher, a Trauma Release Therapy Master Practitioner and Teacher, a Whole Wellness Consultant, Shaman, Aromatherapy Specialist and Host of the Empowering Transformation with Regina Ann Radio Show on Inner Child Radio. Regina Ann is blessed to have been reunited with her Twin Flame Soul Mate, Rich Bentz. Together they create a safe and loving home for their sons.

The artist, Regina Ann, is a published author of three books. "Optimize U" is a self-optimization book designed to bring balance to your life. "Optimize U – Upgrade 2011" is the updated version of the original with new tools and tips. "Poetic Essences…a journey into the beautiful" is a compilation of poetry and divine inspired messages penned over and 18 month period. Along with writing, Regina Ann sings with a local band, draws, paints and enjoys graphic design.

On a Passionate Mission to heal humanity, Regina Ann will ever focus on opportunities that allow her to assist and facilitate healing for all people.

(918) 695-5876

Resonance.ReginaAnn@gmail.com
http://ResonanceHealing.yolasite.com

a few words from... Regina Ann

It is my honor to speak about the beautiful soul that is "just bill". I became friends with Bill through our poetry. I saw in his poetry sparks of light that resonated with mine and I suddenly felt less alone in the darkness that once was my world. He reached out to me with a *maitri* love that I had not experienced save in my dreams. He has ever encouraged me as I, empowered, journey through my transforming.

The beauty of Bill's works, including this one, is the transparency of his heart. In bearing his poetic soul he welcomes you in and bids you feel at home. Disarming the locked doors and shuttered windows to your inner child, Bill reveals the freedom, the joy, and the love that exists in vulnerability.

The Vine Keeper is a beautiful collection of poetic prose that journeys through ego, higher self, angels and Divine. May you soar to new heights as you allow the penned lines of The Vine Keeper to inscribe themselves onto your heart.

Regina Ann
Resonant Renaissance Woman

Resonance Healing
Empowering Transformation with Regina Ann Radio Show

Martina Reisz Newberry is the author of seven books of poetry, the most recent of which are Learning by Rote (Deerbrook Press), and 100 Select Poems Plus One (Inner Child Press). Newberry has been included in *Ascent Aspirations* first two hard-copy Anthologies, also in the anthologies *In The Company Of Women* and *Blessed Are These Hands*. She has been widely published in literary magazines such as: *Pedestal Magazine, Connecticut Poetry Review, Cenacle, Counterpunch, Divine Femme, Istanbul Literary Review, Southern Review of Poetry, Shot of Ink* and others.

More information available at: http://www.martinanewberry.com

a few words from . . . Martina Reisz Newberry

William S. Peters, Sr.'s work never fails to give my heart and soul something to think about. His devotion to poetry and his solid belief in the power of poets to change the world is the strongest I've ever encountered. His work exemplifies this life focus with every poem. In this new book, the following words stay with me:

"…and the Cock still

does what he does

all through the night now

and the quandary still prevails

what ails man

that he can not find peace

will the search ever cease

for that which is everlasting."

I am so glad he's gifted us with this new work and grateful every day for knowing him.

Martina Reisz Newberry
Author, Friend

Bill Douglas, Founder of World Healing Day and World Tai Chi & Qigong Day, author of a best-selling tai chi book, "The Complete Idiot's Guide to T'ai Chi & Qigong," and an award winning novelist, including "2012 The Awakening," and "A Conspiracy of Spirits."

http://worldhealingday.org/

a few words from . . . *Bill Douglass*

William S. Peters, Sr. is a tidal force for compassion and hope. His work is dedicated to shining light on the best in those he discovers who are fostering human evolution and love. Bill has the ability to lift those people and inspire them to become even more than they were when he discovered them.

Bill Douglas

World Healing Day
http://worldhealingday.org/

Teresa E. Gallion moved to New Mexico in 1987. She completed her undergraduate work at University of Illinois Chicago and her Masters Degree in Psychology from Bowling Green State University in Ohio. She recently retired from New Mexico state government.

She has been writing sporadically since the 1970s. She started reading her work in the New Mexico poetry community in 1998. She has been a featured reader at local coffee houses, art galleries, museums, libraries, Outpost Performance Space and the Route 66 Festival in 2001. She occasionally hosts an open mic.

Teresa's work is published in numerous Journals and anthologies. She has a chapbook, *Walking Sacred Ground* and a CD, *On the Wings of the Wind*. Her most recent book *is Contemplation in the High Desert (quatrains inspired by the poetry of Rumi)*. The surreal high desert landscape and her personal spiritual journey influence the writing. When she is not writing, she is committed to hiking the enchanted landscapes of New Mexico.

You may preview her work at
http://teresagallion.yolasite.com and http://www.cdbaby.com/cd/gallionhall.

a few words from . . . *Teresa E. Gallion*

William S. Peters Sr. writes from the heart of a seeker. The renderings in this work are both spiritual and philosophical at many levels and raw with life's hardcore realities. They commit the reader to introspective considerations of the highs and lows in our life cycles. The Vine Keeper may be viewed as a metaphor for growth and awakening as we experience the positive and negative rain on our pathways.

A light of hope floats incognito throughout the book. The poem, *the vine keeper* sets a tone of humility in the powerful stanza:

> *my hands which knead forth promise*
> *are covered with the fragrance of the earth*
> *whose thirst is filled*
> *by the sweat of my brow*

Humility is shelved aside as the seeker questions the purpose of greed, anger, war, death, hunger and abuse in the community of mankind. The seeker comes to a state of gratitude woven into the fabric of this work. The poem, *can i hear that call* tells us:

> *he sat in an ambient silence*
> *as he awaited the dawn of this day's symphony*
> *where the fragrance of Mother's offering*
> *danced in the gentle stirring*
> *of life*

Mr. Peters is the Vine Keeper pondering the questions we all seek to answer and he takes us on his journey through the light and dark side of life. Come and walk with the Vine Keeper.

Teresa E. Gallion, Poet
Author of Contemplation in the High Desert

EXPERIENCE Founder, Speaker Shamshir Rai Luthra (Śamaśīra Rāya Lutharā) is a welfare activist who has the courage to change conventions and set trends. In 1994, he led the way in speaking 'bolchaal bhasha' (the common man's language) on air! He succeeded as content consultant & voice trainer in Nepal in 1996, way ahead of India's second radio boom. In 1997, he awakened the need for self confidence, personality development & voice training for each Indian. He authored two books, 'Talk To Win' in 2002 and 'Lazy Ways To Enlightenment' in 2003. At the peak of an action-packed career in media, renowned broadcaster and celebrity coach Shamshir Rai Luthra sensed an emergent need to spread the message of constructive thinking and good communication everywhere. Consequently, he founded Talking Rich in 2006, and Ashirvachan in 2010.

IDEOLOGY "I will speak for trees, the birds, and the bees…" highlights his concern for mother nature. He has made a sincere effort to work towards the betterment of humanity in any manner possible and continues to do so. In 1998, he was selected as a United Nations Volunteer in an All India Talent Search for Grass Root Leaders which was jointly evaluated by The United Nations Development Program and The Gandhi Peace Foundation. Since his school days, he has conducted numerous tree plantation drives across neighborhoods, written articles on environment protection, managed nature clubs for WWF India, raised funds and volunteered for organizations such as Consumers Forum, Amnesty International, CUTS, Centre for U.N. Studies, Deepalaya, Cry, Blind Relief Association Of India, the Red Cross Society, etc.

http://shamshirrailuthra.org/
http://www.flipkart.com/search-books?query=shamshir+rai+luthra&field=author

a few words from... Shamshir Rai Luthra

Every poem by William S. Peters Sr. that I have read, I have imagined it being spoken in his golden voice.

Read his poems when your mind is restless, and you shall find great strength to calm it. Read them with a relaxed mind, and you shall fathom and commune with his simple, straight-forward, and beautiful soul.

Shamshir Rai Luthra

http://shamshirrailuthra.org/

other Titles by . . . *Bill*

the Wind, the Mountain and the Sage
photo ~ poetry ~ spiritual

This Too Shall Pass
poetry

The Light In The Window
poetry

The Book of 'i'
poetry

my inner garden
poetry

Good Morning My Beloved Family
sayings & witticisms

Free Thinker
spoken word CD

available at :

http://www.iamjustbill.com/bills-market.php

http://www.innerchildpress.com/the-book-store.php

Inner Child Press

Inner Child Press is a Publishing Company Founded and Operated by Writers. Our personal publishing experiences provides us an intimate understanding of the sometimes daunting challenges Writers, New and Seasoned may face in the Business of Publishing and Marketing their Creative "Written Work".

For more Information

Inner Child Press

www.innerchildpress.com

~ fini ~

www.ingramcontent.com/pod-product-compliance
Lightning Source LLC
Chambersburg PA
CBHW081208230426
43666CB00015B/2675